Mary, Queen of Scots

# Mary, Queen of Scots

Makers of History Series

Jacob Abbott

Cedar Lake Classics

Copyright © 2023 by Cedar Lake Classics

This is an annotated edition of a public domain work.

# CONTENTS

PHOTO INSERT vii
PREFACE ix

1 Mary's Childhood 1

2 Her Education in France 16

3 The Great Wedding 27

4 Misfortunes 39

5 Return to Scotland 52

6 Mary and Lord Darnley 66

7 Rizzio 79

8 Bothwell 92

9 The Fall of Bothwell 108

10 Loch Leven Castle 120

11 The Long Captivity 135

12 The End 144

# CONTENTS

ABOUT JACOB ABBOTT **159**
BIOGRAPHIES ABBOTT WROTE **161**

Mary Queen of Scots in Captivity

# PREFACE

THE history of the life of every individual who has, for any reason, attracted extensively the attention of mankind, has been written in a great variety of ways by a multitude of authors, and persons sometimes wonder why we should have so many different accounts of the same thing. The reason is, that each one of these accounts is intended for a different set of readers, who read with ideas and purposes widely dissimilar from each other. Among the twenty millions of people in the United States, there are perhaps two millions, between the ages of fifteen and twenty-five, who wish to become acquainted, in general, with the leading events in the history of the Old World, and of ancient times, but who, coming upon the stage in this land and at this period, have ideas and conceptions so widely different from those of other nations and of other times, that a mere republication of existing accounts is not what they require. The story must be told expressly for them. The things that are to be explained, the points that are to be brought out, the comparative degree of prominence to be given to the various particulars, will all be different, on account of the difference in the situation, the ideas, and the objects of these new readers, compared with those of the various other classes of readers which former authors have had in view. It is for this reason, and with this view, that the present series of historical narratives is presented to the public. The author, having had some opportunity to become acquainted with the position, the ideas, and the intellectual wants of those whom he addresses, presents the result of his labors to them, with the hope that it may be found successful in accomplishing its design.

## PREFACE

Dumbarton Castle, on the Clyde. Painting by Henry Bright.

# 1

## Mary's Childhood

### 1542-1548

*Palace where Mary was born.—Its situation.—Ruins.—The room.—Visitors.—Mary's father in the wars.—His death.—Regency.—Catholic religion.—The Protestants.—England and France.—The Earl of Arran.—The regency.—Arran regent.—New plan.—End of the war.—King Henry VIII.—Janet Sinclair.—King Henry's demands.—Objections to them.—Plans for Mary.—Linlithgow.—Plan of the palace.—Fountain.—The lion's den.—Explanation of the engraving.—The coronation.—Stirling Castle.—Its situation.—Rocky hill.—The coronation scene.—Linlithgow and Stirling.—The Highlands and the Highlanders.—Religious disturbances.—Lake Menteith.—Mary's companions.—The four Maries.—Angry disputes.—Change of plan.—Henry's anger.—Henry's sickness and death.—War renewed.—Danger in Edinburgh.—Aid from France.—New plan.—Going to France.—Dumbarton Castle.—Rock of Dumbarton.—Journey to Dumbarton.—The four Maries.—Departure from Scotland.*

TRAVELERS who go into Scotland take a great interest in visiting, among other places, a certain room in the ruins of an old palace, where Queen Mary was born. Queen Mary was very beautiful, but she was very unfortunate and unhappy. Every body takes a strong interest in her story, and this interest attaches, in some degree, to the room where her sad and sorrowful life was begun.

The palace is near a little village called Linlithgow. The village has but one long street, which consists of ancient stone houses. North of it is a little lake, or rather pond: they call it, in Scotland, a *loch*. The palace is between the village and the loch; it is upon a beautiful swell of land which projects out into the water. There is a very small island in the middle of the loch and the shores are bordered with fertile fields. The palace, when entire, was square, with an open space or court in the center. There was a beautiful stone fountain in the center of this court, and an arched gateway through which horsemen and carriages could ride in. The doors of entrance into the palace were on the inside of the court.

The palace is now in ruins. A troop of soldiers came to it one day in time of war, after Mary and her mother had left it, and spent the night there: they spread straw over the floors to sleep upon. In the morning, when they went away, they wantonly set the straw on fire, and left it burning, and thus the palace was destroyed. Some of the lower floors were of stone; but all the upper floors and the roof were burned, and all the wood-work of the rooms, and the doors and window-frames. Since then the palace has never been repaired, but remains a melancholy pile of ruins.

The room where Mary was born had a stone floor. The rubbish which has fallen from above has covered it with a sort of soil, and grass and weeds grow up all over it. It is a very melancholy sight to see. The visitors who go into the room walk mournfully about, trying to imagine how Queen Mary looked, as an infant in her mother's arms, and reflecting on the recklessness of the soldiers in wantonly destroying so beautiful a palace. Then they go to the window, or, rather, to the crumbling opening in the wall where the window once was, and look out upon the loch, now so deserted and lonely; over their heads it is all open to the sky.

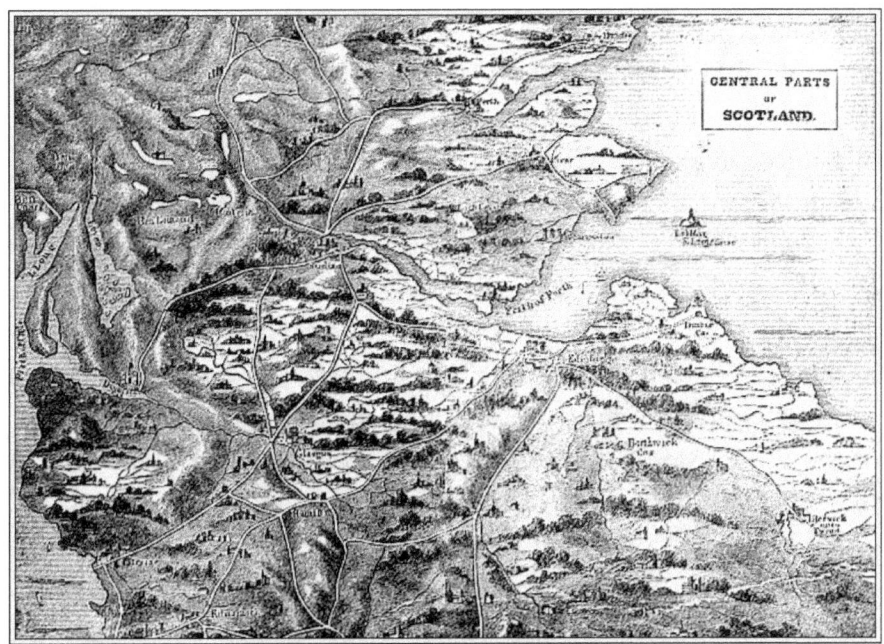

Map of the Central Part of Scotland

Mary's father was King of Scotland. At the time that Mary was born, he was away from home engaged in war with the King of England, who had invaded Scotland. In the battles Mary's father was defeated, and he thought that the generals and nobles who commanded his army allowed the English to conquer them on purpose to betray him. This thought overwhelmed him with vexation and anguish. He pined away under the acuteness of his sufferings, and just after the news came to him that his daughter Mary was born, he died. Thus Mary became an orphan, and her troubles commenced, at the very beginning of her days. She never saw her father, and her father never saw her. Her mother was a French lady; her name was Mary of Guise. Her own name was Mary Stuart, but she is commonly called Mary Queen of Scots.

As Mary was her father's only child, of course, when he died, she became Queen of Scotland, although she was only a few days old. It is customary, in such a case, to appoint some distinguished person to govern the kingdom, in the name of the young queen, until she grows up: such a person is called a *regent*. Mary's mother wished to be the regent until Mary became of age.

It happened that in those days, as now, the government and people of France were of the Catholic religion. England, on the other hand, was Protestant. There is a great difference between the Catholic and the Protestant systems. The Catholic Church, though it extends nearly all over the world, is banded together, as the reader is aware, under one man—the pope—who is the great head of the Church, and who lives in state at Rome. The Catholics have, in all countries, many large and splendid churches, which are ornamented with paintings and images of the Virgin Mary and of Christ. They perform great ceremonies in these churches, the priests being dressed in magnificent costumes, and walking in processions, with censers of incense burning as they go. The Protestants, on the other hand, do not like these ceremonies; they regard such outward acts of worship as mere useless parade, and the images as idols. They themselves have smaller and plainer churches, and call the people together in them to hear sermons, and to offer up simple prayers.

In the time of Mary, England was Protestant and France was Catholic, while Scotland was divided, though most of the people were Protestants. The two parties were very much excited against each other, and often persecuted each other with extreme cruelty. Sometimes the Protestants would break into the Catholic churches, and tear down and destroy the paintings and the images, and the other symbols of worship, all which the Catholics regarded with extreme veneration; this exasperated the Catholics, and when they became powerful in their turn, they would seize the Protestants and imprison them, and sometimes burn them to death, by tying them to a stake and piling fagots of wood about them, and then setting the heap on fire.

Queen Mary's mother was a Catholic, and for that reason the people of Scotland were not willing that she should be regent. There were one or two other persons, moreover, who claimed the office. One was a certain nobleman called the Earl of Arran. He was a Protestant. The

Earl of Arran was the next heir to the crown, so that if Mary had died in her infancy, he would have been king. He thought that this was a reason why *he* should be regent, and govern the kingdom until Mary became old enough to govern it herself. Many other persons, however, considered this rather a reason why he should not be regent; for they thought he would be naturally interested in wishing that Mary should not live, since if she died he would himself become king, and that therefore he would not be a safe protector for her. However, as the Earl of Arran was a Protestant, and as Mary's mother was a Catholic, and as the Protestant interest was the strongest, it was at length decided that Arran should be the regent, and govern the country until Mary should be of age.

It is a curious circumstance that Mary's birth put an end to the war between England and Scotland, and that in a very singular way. The King of England had been fighting against Mary's father, James, for a long time, in order to conquer the country and annex it to England; and now that James was dead, and Mary had become queen, with Arran for the regent, it devolved on Arran to carry on the war. But the King of England and his government, now that the young queen was born, conceived of a new plan. The king had a little son, named Edward, about four years old, who, of course, would become King of England in his place when he should himself die. Now he thought it would be best for him to conclude a peace with Scotland, and agree with the Scottish government that, as soon as Mary was old enough, she should become Edward's wife, and the two kingdoms be united in that way.

The name of this King of England was Henry the Eighth. He was a very headstrong and determined man. This, his plan, might have been a very good one; it was certainly much better than an attempt to get possession of Scotland by fighting for it; but he was very far from being as moderate and just as he should have been in the execution of his design. The first thing was to ascertain whether Mary was a strong and healthy child; for if he should make a treaty of peace, and give up all his plans of conquest, and then if Mary, after living feebly a few years, should die, all his plans would fail. To satisfy him on this point, they actually had some of the infant's clothes removed in the presence of his embassador, in order that the embassador might see that her form was perfect, and her limbs vigorous and strong. The nurse did this with great pride and pleasure, Mary's mother standing by. The nurse's name was Janet Sinclair. The embassador wrote back to Henry, the King of England, that little Mary was "as goodly a child as he ever saw." So King Henry VIII. was confirmed in his design of having her for the wife of his son.

King Henry VIII. accordingly changed all his plans. He made a peace with the Earl of Arran. He dismissed the prisoners that he had taken, and sent them home kindly. If he had been contented with kind and gentle measures like these, he might have succeeded in them, although there was, of course, a strong party in Scotland opposed to them. Mary's mother was opposed to them, for she was a Catholic and a French lady, and she wished to have her daughter become a Catholic as she grew up, and marry a French prince. All the Catholics in Scotland took her side. Still Henry's plans might have been accomplished, perhaps, if he had been moderate and conciliating in the efforts which he made to carry them into effect.

But Henry VIII. was headstrong and obstinate. He demanded that Mary, since she was to be his son's wife, should be given up to him to be taken into England, and educated there, under the care of persons whom he should appoint. He also demanded that the Parliament of Scotland should let him have a large share in the government of Scotland, because he was going to be the father-in-law of the young queen. The Parliament would not agree to either of these plans; they were entirely unwilling to allow their little queen to be carried off to another country, and put under the charge of so rough and rude a man. Then they were unwilling, too, to give him any share of the government during Mary's minority. Both these measures were entirely inadmissible; they would, if adopted, have put both the infant Queen of Scotland and the kingdom itself completely in the power of one who had always been their greatest enemy.

# MARY, QUEEN OF SCOTS

Henry, finding that he could not induce the Scotch government to accede to these plans, gave them up at last, and made a treaty of marriage between his son and Mary, with the agreement that she might remain in Scotland until she was ten years old, and that *then* she should come to England and be under his care.

All this time, while these grand negotiations were pending between two mighty nations about her marriage, little Mary was unconscious of it all, sometimes reposing quietly in Janet Sinclair's arms, sometimes looking out of the windows of the Castle of Linlithgow to see the swans swim upon the lake, and sometimes, perhaps, creeping about upon the palace floor, where the earls and barons who came to visit her mother, clad in armor of steel, looked upon her with pride and pleasure. The palace where she lived was beautifully situated, as has been before remarked, on the borders of a lake. It was arranged somewhat in the following manner:

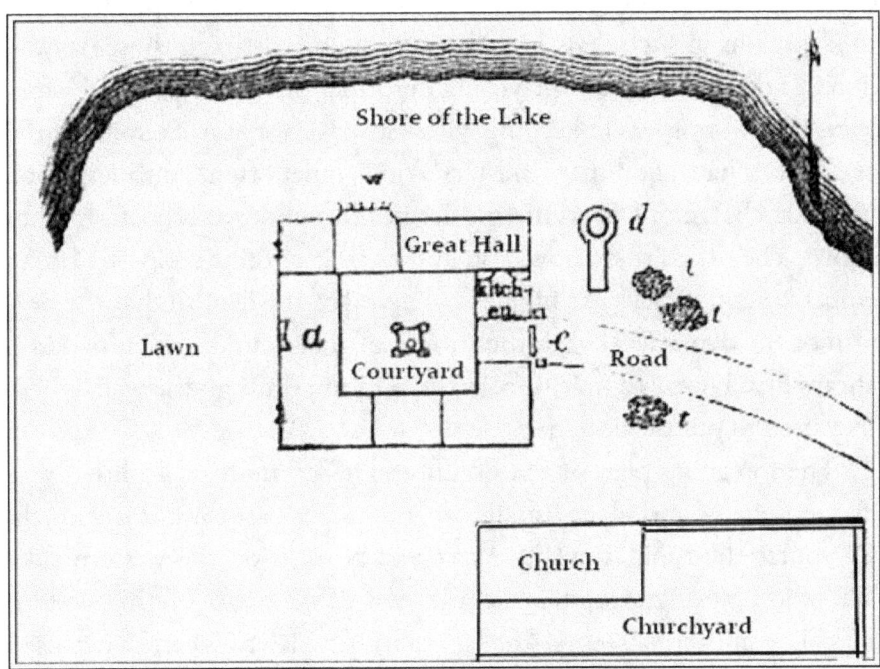

Plan of the Palace of Linlithgow

a. Room where Mary was born.

b. Entrance through great gates.

c. Bow-window projecting toward the water.

d. Den where they kept a lion.

e. *(t)* Trees.

There was a beautiful fountain in the center of the court-yard, where water spouted out from the mouths of carved images, and fell into marble basins below. The ruins of this fountain and of the images remain there still. The den at *d* was a round pit, like a well, which you could look down into from above: it was about ten feet deep. They used to keep lions in such dens near the palaces and castles in those days. A lion in a den was a sort of plaything in former times, as a parrot or a pet lamb is now: this was in keeping with the fierce and warlike spirit of the age. If they had a lion there in Mary's time, Janet often, doubtless, took her little charge out to see it, and let her throw down food to it from above. The den is there now. You approach it upon the top of a broad embankment, which is as high as the depth of the den, so that the bottom of the den is level with the surface of the ground, which makes it always dry. There is a hole, too, at the bottom, through the wall, where they used to put the lion in.

The foregoing plan of the buildings and grounds of Linlithgow is drawn as maps and plans usually are, the upper part toward the north. Of course the room *a*, where Mary was born, is on the western side. The adjoining engraving represents a view of the palace on this western side. The church is seen at the right; and the lawn, where Janet used to take Mary out to breathe the air, is in the fore-ground. The shore of the lake is very near, and winds beautifully around the margin of the promontory on which the palace stands. Of course the lion's den, and the ancient avenue of approach to the palace, are round upon the other side, and out of sight in this view. The approach to the palace, at the present day, is on the southern side, between the church and the trees on the right of the picture.

Palace of Linlithgow—Queen Mary's Birth-place

Mary remained here at Linlithgow for a year or two; but when she was about nine months old, they concluded to have the great ceremony of the coronation performed, as she was by that time old enough to bear the journey to Stirling Castle, where the Scottish kings and queens were generally crowned. The coronation of a queen is an event which always excites a very deep and universal interest among all persons in the realm; and there is a peculiar interest felt when, as was the case in this instance, the queen to be crowned is an infant just old enough to bear the journey. There was a very great interest felt in Mary's coronation. The different courts and monarchs of Europe sent embassadors to be present at the ceremony, and to pay their respects to the infant queen; and Stirling became, for the time being, the center of universal attraction.

Stirling is in the very heart of Scotland. It is a castle, built upon a rock, or, rather, upon a rocky hill, which rises like an island out of the midst of a vast region of beautiful and fertile country, rich and verdant beyond description. Beyond the confines of this region of beauty, dark mountains rise on all sides; and wherever you are, whether riding along the roads in the plain, or climbing the declivities of the mountains, you see Stirling Castle, from every point, capping its rocky hill, the center and ornament of the broad expanse of beauty which surrounds it.

Stirling Castle is north of Linlithgow, and is distant about fifteen or twenty miles from it. The road to it lies not far from the shores of the Frith of Forth, a broad and beautiful sheet of water. The castle, as has been before remarked, was on the summit of a rocky hill. There are precipitous crags on three sides of the hill, and a gradual approach by a long ascent on the fourth side. At the top of this ascent you enter the great gates of the castle, crossing a broad and deep ditch by means of a draw-bridge. You enter then a series of paved courts, with towers and walls around them, and finally come to the more interior edifices, where the private apartments are situated, and where the little queen was crowned.

It was an occasion of great pomp and ceremony, though Mary, of course, was unconscious of the meaning of it all. She was surrounded by barons and earls, by embassadors and princes from foreign courts, and by the principal lords and ladies of the Scottish nobility, all dressed in magnificent costumes. They held little Mary up, and a cardinal, that is, a great dignitary of the Roman Catholic Church, placed the crown upon her head. Half pleased with the glittering show, and half frightened at the strange faces which she saw every where around her, she gazed unconsciously upon the scene, while her mother, who could better understand its import, was elated with pride and joy.

Linlithgow and Stirling are in the open and cultivated part of Scotland. All the northern and western part of the country consists of vast masses of mountains, with dark and somber glens among them, which are occupied solely by shepherds and herdsmen with their flocks and herds. This mountainous region was called the Highlands, and the inhabitants of it were the Highlanders. They were a wild and warlike class of men, and their country was seldom visited by either friend or foe. At the present time there are beautiful roads all through the Highlands, and stage-coaches and private carriages roll over them every summer, to take tourists to see and admire the picturesque and beautiful scenery; but in the days of Mary the whole region was gloomy and desolate, and almost inaccessible.

Mary remained in Linlithgow and Stirling for about two years, and then, as the country was becoming more and more disturbed by the struggles of the great contending parties—those who were in favor of the Catholic religion and alliance with France on the one hand, and of those in favor of the Protestant religion and alliance with England on the other hand—they concluded to send her into the Highlands for safety.

It was not far into the country of the Highlands that they concluded to send her, but only into the *borders* of it. There was a small lake on the southern margin of the wild and mountainous country, called the Lake of Menteith. In this lake was an island named Inchmahome, the word *inch* being the name for island in the language spoken by the Highlanders. This island, which was situated in a very secluded and solitary region, was selected as Mary's place of residence. She was about four years old when they sent her to this place. Several persons went with her to take care of her, and to teach her. In fact, every thing was provided for her which could secure her improvement and happiness. Her mother did not forget that she would need playmates, and so she selected four little girls of about the same age with the little queen herself, and invited them to accompany her. They were daughters of the noblemen and high officers about the court. It is very singular that these girls were all named Mary. Their names in full were as follows:

- Mary Beaton,

- Mary Fleming,

- Mary Livingstone,

- Mary Seaton.

These, with Mary Stuart, which was Queen Mary's name, made five girls of four or five years of age, all named Mary.

Mary lived two years in this solitary island. She had, however, all the comforts and conveniences of life, and enjoyed herself with her four Maries very much. Of course she knew nothing, and thought nothing of the schemes and plans of the great governments for having her married, when she grew up, to the young English prince, who was then a little boy of about her own age, nor of the angry disputes in Scotland to which this subject gave rise. It did give rise to very serious disputes. Mary's mother did not like the plan at all. As she was herself a French lady and a Catholic, she did not wish to have her daughter marry a prince who was of the English royal family, and a Protestant. All the Catholics in Scotland took her side. At length the Earl of Arran, who was the regent, changed to that side; and finally the government, being thus brought over, gave notice to King Henry VIII. that the plan must be given up, as they had concluded, on the whole, that Mary should not marry his son.

King Henry was very much incensed. He declared that Mary *should* marry his son, and he raised an army and sent it into Scotland to make war upon the Scotch again, and compel them to consent to the execution of the plan. He was at this time beginning to be sick, but his sickness, instead of softening his temper, only made him the more ferocious and cruel. He turned against his best friends. He grew worse, and was evidently about to die; but he was so irritable and angry that for a long time no one dared to tell him of his approaching dissolution, and he lay restless, and wretched, and agitated with political animosities upon his dying bed. At length some one ventured to tell him that his end was near. When he found that he must die, he resigned himself to his fate. He sent for an archbishop to come and see him, but he was speechless when the prelate came, and soon afterward expired.

The English government, however, after his death, adhered to his plan of compelling the Scotch to make Mary the wife of his son. They sent an army into Scotland. A great battle was fought, and the Scotch were defeated. The battle was fought at a place not far from Edinburgh, and near the sea. It was so near the sea that the English fired upon the Scotch army from their ships, and thus assisted their troops upon the shore. The armies had remained several days near each other before coming to battle, and during all this time the city of Edinburgh was in a state of great anxiety and suspense, as they expected that their city would be attacked by the English if they should conquer in the battle. The English army did, in fact, advance toward Edinburgh after the battle was over, and would have got possession of it had it not been for the castle. There is a very strong castle in the very heart of Edinburgh, upon the summit of a rocky hill.

These attempts of the English to force the Scotch government to consent to Mary's marriage only made them the more determined to prevent it. A great many who were not opposed to it before, became opposed to it now when they saw foreign armies in the country destroying the towns and murdering the people. They said they had no great objection to the match, but that they did not like the mode of wooing. They sent to France to ask the French king to send over an army to aid them, and promised him that if he would do so they would agree that Mary should marry *his* son. His son's name was Francis.

The French king was very much pleased with this plan. He sent an army of six thousand men into Scotland to assist the Scotch against their English enemies. It was arranged, also, as little Mary was now hardly safe among all these commotions, even in her retreat in the island of Inchmahome, to send her to France to be educated there, and to live there until she was old enough to be married. The same ships which brought the army from France to Scotland, were to carry Mary and her retinue from Scotland to France. The four Maries went with her.

They bade their lonely island farewell, and traveled south till they came to a strong castle on a high, rocky hill, on the banks of the River

Clyde. The name of this fortress is Dumbarton Castle. Almost all the castles of those times were built upon precipitous hills, to increase the difficulties of the enemies in approaching them. The Rock of Dumbarton is a very remarkable one. It stands close to the bank of the river. There are a great many ships and steam-boats continually passing up and down the Clyde, to and from the great city of Glasgow, and all the passengers on board gaze with great interest, as they sail by, on the Rock of Dumbarton, with the castle walls on the sides, and the towers and battlements crowning the summit. In Mary's time there was comparatively very little shipping on the river, but the French fleet was there, waiting opposite the castle to receive Mary and the numerous persons who were to go in her train. [Travelers who visit Scotland from this country at the present day, usually land first, at the close of the voyage across the Atlantic, at Liverpool, and there take a Glasgow steamer. Glasgow, which is the great commercial city of Scotland, is on the River Clyde. This river flows northward to the sea. The steamer, in ascending the river, makes its way with difficulty along the narrow channel, which, besides being narrow and tortuous, is obstructed by boats, ships, steamers, and every other variety of water-craft, such as are always going to and fro in the neighborhood of any great commercial emporium. The tourists, who stand upon the deck gazing at this exciting scene of life and motion, have their attention strongly attracted, about half way up the river, by this Castle of Dumbarton, which crowns a rocky hill, rising abruptly from the water's edge, on the north side of the stream. It attracts sometimes the more attention from American travelers, on account of its being the first ancient castle they see. This it likely to be the case if they proceed to Scotland immediately on landing at Liverpool.]

Mary was escorted from the island where she had been living, across the country to Dumbarton Castle, with a strong retinue. She was now between five and six years of age. She was, of course, too young to know any thing about the contentions and wars which had distracted her country on her account, or to feel much interest in the subject of her approaching departure from her native land. She enjoyed the novelty of the scenes through which she passed on her journey. She was pleased with the dresses and the arms of the soldiers who accompanied her, and with the ships which were floating in the river, beneath the walls of the Castle of Dumbarton, when she arrived there. She was pleased, too, to think that, wherever she was to go, her four Maries were to go with her. She bade her mother farewell, embarked on board the ship which was to receive her, and sailed away from her native land, not to return to it again for many years.

# 2

## Her Education in France

### 1548-1556

*Departure.—Stormy voyage.—Journey to Paris.—Release of prisoners.—Barabbas.—St. Germain.—Celebrations.—The convent.—Character of the nuns.—Interest in Mary.—Leaving the convent.—Amusements.—Visit of Mary's mother.—Queen dowager.—Rouen.—A happy meeting.—Rejoicings.—A last farewell.—Visit to a mourner.—The queen dowager's return.—The regency.—A page of honor.—Sir James Melville.—Mary's character.—Her diligence.—Devices and mottoes.—Festivities.—Water parties.—Hunting.—An accident.—Restraint.—Queen Catharine.—Her character.—Embroidery.—Mary's admiration of Queen Catharine.—The latter suspicious.—Unguarded remark.—Catharine's mortification.—The dauphin.—Origin of the title.—Character of Francis.—Mary's beauty.—Torch-light procession.—An angel.—Mary a Catholic.—Her conscientiousness and fidelity.*

THE departure of Mary from Scotland, little as she was, was a great event both for Scotland and for France. In those days kings and queens were even of greater relative importance than they are now, and all Scotland was interested in the young queen's going away from them, and all France in expecting her arrival. She sailed down the Clyde, and then passed along the seas and channels which lie between England and

Ireland. These seas, though they look small upon the map, are really spacious and wide, and are often greatly agitated by winds and storms. This was the case at the time Mary made her voyage. The days and nights were tempestuous and wild, and the ships had difficulty in keeping in each other's company. There was danger of being blown upon the coasts, or upon the rocks or islands which lie in the way. Mary was too young to give much heed to these dangers, but the lords and commissioners, and the great ladies who went to attend her, were heartily glad when the voyage was over. It ended safely at last, after several days of tossing upon the stormy billows, by their arrival upon the northern coast of France. They landed at a town called Brest.

The King of France had made great preparations for receiving the young queen immediately upon her landing. Carriages and horses had been provided to convey herself and the company of her attendants, by easy journeys, to Paris. They received her with great pomp and ceremony at every town which she passed through. One mark of respect which they showed her was very singular. The king ordered that every prison which she passed in her route should be thrown open, and the prisoners set free. This fact is a striking illustration of the different ideas which prevailed in those days, compared with those which are entertained now, in respect to crime and punishment. Crime is now considered as an offense against the *community*, and it would be considered no favor to the community, but the reverse, to let imprisoned criminals go free. In those days, on the other hand, crimes were considered rather as injuries committed *by* the community, and against the king; so that, if the monarch wished to show the community a favor, he would do it by releasing such of them as had been imprisoned by his officers for their crimes. It was just so in the time of our Savior, when the Jews had a custom of having some criminal released to them once a year, at the Passover, by the Roman government, as an act of *favor*. That is, the government was accustomed to furnish, by way of contributing its share toward the general festivities of the occasion, the setting of a robber and a murderer at liberty!

The King of France has several palaces in the neighborhood of Paris. Mary was taken to one of them, named St. Germain. This palace, which still stands, is about twelve miles from Paris, toward the northwest. It is a very magnificent residence, and has been for many centuries a favorite resort of the French kings. Many of them were born in it. There are extensive parks and gardens connected with it, and a great artificial forest, in which the trees were all planted and cultivated like the trees of an orchard. Mary was received at this palace with great pomp and parade; and many spectacles and festivities were arranged to amuse her and the four Maries who accompanied her, and to impress her strongly with an idea of the wealth, and power, and splendor of the great country to which she had come.

She remained here but a short time, and then it was arranged for her to go to a *convent* to be educated. Convents were in those days, as in fact they are now, quite famous as places of education. They were situated sometimes in large towns, and sometimes in secluded places in the country; but, whether in town or country, the inmates of them were shut up very strictly from all intercourse with the world. They were under the care of nuns who had devoted themselves for life to the service. These nuns were some of them unhappy persons, who were weary of the sorrows and sufferings of the world, and who were glad to retire from it to such a retreat as they fancied the convent would be. Others became nuns from conscientious principles of duty, thinking that they should commend themselves to the favor of God by devoting their lives to works of benevolence and to the exercises of religion. Of course there were all varieties of character among the nuns; some of them were selfish and disagreeable, others were benevolent and kind.

At the convent where Mary was sent there were some nuns of very excellent and amiable character, and they took a great interest in Mary, both because she was a queen, and because she was beautiful, and of a kind and affectionate disposition. Mary became very strongly attached to these nuns, and began to entertain the idea of becoming a nun herself, and spending her life with them in the convent. It seemed pleasant to her to live there in such a peaceful seclusion, in company with those who loved her, and whom she herself loved, but the King of France, and the Scottish nobles who had come with her from Scotland, would, of course, be opposed to any such plan. They intended her to be married to the young prince, and to become one of the great ladies of the court, and to lead a life of magnificence and splendor. They became alarmed, therefore, when they found that she was imbibing a taste for the life of seclusion and solitude which is led by a nun. They decided to take her immediately away.

Mary bade farewell to the convent and its inmates with much regret and many tears; but, notwithstanding her reluctance, she was obliged to submit. If she had not been a queen, she might, perhaps, have had her own way. As it was, however, she was obliged to leave the convent and the nuns whom she loved, and to go back to the palaces of the king, in which she afterward continued to live, sometimes in one and sometimes in another, for many years. Wherever she went, she was surrounded with scenes of great gayety and splendor. They wished to obliterate from her mind all recollections of the convent, and all love of solitude and seclusion. They did not neglect her studies, but they filled up the intervals of study with all possible schemes of enjoyment and pleasure, to amuse and occupy her mind and the minds of her companions. Her companions were her own four Maries, and the two daughters of the French king.

When Mary was about seven years of age, that is, after she had been two years in France, her mother formed a plan to come from Scotland to see her. Her mother had remained behind when Mary left Scotland, as she had an important part to perform in public affairs, and in the administration of the government of Scotland while Mary was away. She wanted, however, to come and see her. France, too, was her own native land, and all her relations and friends resided there. She wished to see them as well as Mary, and to revisit once more the palaces and cities where her own early life had been spent. In speaking of Mary's mother we shall call her sometimes the queen dowager. The expression *queen dowager* is the one usually applied to the widow of a king, as *queen consort* is used to denote the *wife* of a king.

This visit of the queen dowager of Scotland to her little daughter in France was an event of great consequence, and all the arrangements for carrying it into effect were conducted with great pomp and ceremony. A large company attended her, with many of the Scottish lords and ladies among them. The King of France, too, went from Paris toward the French coast, to meet the party of visitors, taking little Mary and a large company of attendants with him. They went to Rouen, a large city not far from the coast, where they awaited the arrival of Mary's mother, and where they received her with great ceremonies of parade and rejoicing. The queen regent was very much delighted to see her little daughter again. She had grown two years older, and had improved greatly in every respect, and tears of joy came into her mother's eyes as she clasped her in her arms. The two parties journeyed in company to Paris and entered the city with great rejoicings. The two queens, mother and daughter, were the objects of universal interest and attention. Feasts and celebrations without end were arranged for them, and every possible means of amusement and rejoicing were contrived in the palaces of Paris, of St. Germain's, and of Fontainebleau. Mary's mother remained in France about a year. She then bade Mary farewell, leaving her at Fontainebleau. This proved to be a final farewell, for she never saw her again.

After taking leave of her daughter, the queen dowager went, before leaving France, to see her own mother, who was a widow, and who was living at a considerable distance from Paris in seclusion, and in a state of austere and melancholy grief, on account of the loss of her husband. Instead of forgetting her sorrows, as she ought to have done, and returning calmly and peacefully to the duties and enjoyments of life, she had given herself up to inconsolable grief, and was doing all she could to perpetuate the mournful influence of her sorrows. She lived in an ancient and gloomy mansion, of vast size, and she had hung all the apartments in black, to make it still more desolate and gloomy, and to continue the influence of grief upon her mind. Here the queen dowager found her, spending her time in prayers and austerities of every kind, making herself and all her family perfectly miserable. Many persons, at the present day, act, under such circumstances, on the same principle and with the same spirit, though they do not do it perhaps in precisely the same way.

One would suppose that Mary's mother would have preferred to remain in France with her daughter and her mother and all her family friends, instead of going back to Scotland, where she was, as it were, a foreigner and a stranger. The reason why she desired to go back was that she wished to be made *queen regent*, and thus have the government of Scotland in her own hands. She would rather be queen regent in Scotland than a simple queen *mother* in France. While she was in France, she urged the king to use all his influence to have Arran resign his regency into her hands, and finally obtained writings from him and from Queen Mary to this effect. She then left France and went to Scotland, going through England on the way. The young King of England, to whom Mary had been engaged by the government when she was an infant in Janet Sinclair's arms, renewed his proposals to the queen dowager to let her daughter become his wife; but she told him that it was all settled that she was to be married to the French prince, and that it was now too late to change the plan.

There was a young gentleman, about nineteen or twenty years of age, who came from Scotland also, not far from this time, to wait upon Mary as her page of honor. A page is an attendant above the rank of an ordinary servant, whose business it is to wait upon his mistress, to read to her, sometimes to convey her letters and notes, and to carry her commands to the other attendants who are beneath him in rank and whose business it is actually to perform the services which the lady requires. A page *of honor* is a young gentleman who sustains this office in a nominal and temporary manner for a princess or a queen.

The name of Mary's page of honor, who came to her now from Scotland, was Sir James Melville. The only reason for mentioning him thus particularly, rather than the many other officers and attendants by whom Mary was surrounded was, that the service which he thus commenced was continued in various ways through the whole period of Mary's life. We shall often hear of him in the subsequent parts of this narrative. He followed Mary to Scotland when she returned to that country, and became afterward her secretary, and also her embassador on many occasions. He was now quite young, and when he landed at Brest he traveled slowly to Paris in the care of two Scotchmen, to whose charge he had been intrusted. He was a young man of uncommon talents and of great accomplishments, and it was a mark of high distinction for him to be appointed page of honor to the queen, although he was about nineteen years of age and she was but seven.

After the queen regent's return to Scotland, Mary went on improving in every respect more and more. She was diligent, industrious, and tractable. She took a great interest in her studies. She was not only beautiful in person, and amiable and affectionate in heart, but she possessed a very intelligent and active mind, and she entered with a sort of quiet but earnest enthusiasm into all the studies to which her attention was called. She paid a great deal of attention to music, to poetry, and to drawing. She used to invent little devices for seals, with French and Latin mottoes, and, after drawing them again and again with great care, until she was satisfied with the design, she would give them to the gem-engravers to be cut upon stone seals, so that she could seal her letters with them. These mottoes and devices can not well be represented in English, as the force and beauty of them depended generally upon a double meaning in some word of French or Latin, which can not be preserved in the translation. We shall, however, give one of these seals, which she made just before she left France, to return to Scotland, when we come to that period of her history.

The King of France, and the lords and ladies who came with Mary from Scotland, contrived a great many festivals and celebrations in the parks, and forests, and palaces, to amuse the queen and the four Maries who were with her. The daughters of the French king joined, also, in these pleasures. They would have little balls, and parties, and pic-nics, sometimes in the open air, sometimes in the little summer-houses built upon the grounds attached to the palaces. The scenes of these festivities were in many cases made unusually joyous and gay by bon-fires and illuminations. They had water parties on the little lakes, and hunting parties through the parks and forests. Mary was a very graceful and beautiful rider, and full of courage. Sometimes she met with accidents which were attended with some danger. Once, while hunting the stag, and riding at full speed with a great company of ladies and gentlemen behind her and before her, her dress got caught by the bough of a tree, and she was pulled to the ground. The horse went on. Several other riders drove by her without seeing her, as she had too much composure and fortitude to attract their attention by outcries and lamentations. They saw her, however, at last, and came to her assistance. They brought back her horse, and, smoothing down her hair, which had fallen into confusion, she mounted again, and rode on after the stag as before.

Notwithstanding all these means of enjoyment and diversion, Mary was subjected to a great deal of restraint. The rules of etiquette are very precise and very strictly enforced in royal households, and they were still more strict in those days than they are now. The king was very ceremonious in all his arrangements, and was surrounded by a multitude of officers who performed every thing by rule. As Mary grew older, she was subjected to greater and greater restraint. She used to spend a considerable portion of every day in the apartments of Queen Catharine, the wife of the King of France and the mother of the little Francis to whom she was to be married. Mary and Queen Catharine did not, however, like each other very well. Catharine was a woman of strong mind and of an imperious disposition; and it is supposed by some that she was jealous of Mary because she was more beautiful and accomplished and more generally beloved than her own daughters, the princesses of France. At any rate, she treated Mary in rather a stern and haughty manner, and it was thought that she would finally oppose her marriage to Francis her son.

And yet Mary was at first very much pleased with Queen Catharine, and was accustomed to look up to her with great admiration, and to feel for her a very sincere regard. She often went into the queen's apartments, where they sat together and talked, or worked upon their embroidery, which was a famous amusement for ladies of exalted rank in those days. Mary herself at one time worked a large piece, which she sent as a present to the nuns in the convent where she had resided; and afterward, in Scotland, she worked a great many things, some of which still remain, and may be seen in her ancient rooms in the palace of Holyrood House. She learned this art by working with Queen Catharine in her apartments. When she first became acquainted with Catharine on these occasions, she used to love her society. She admired her talents and her conversational powers, and she liked very much to be in her room. She listened to all she said, watched her movements, and endeavored in all things to follow her example.

Catharine, however, thought that this was all a pretense, and that Mary did not really like her, but only wished to make her believe that she did so in order to get favor, or to accomplish some other selfish end. One day she asked her why she seemed to prefer her society to that of her youthful and more suitable companions. Mary replied, in substance, "The reason was, that though with them she might enjoy much, she could learn nothing; while she always learned from Queen Catharine's conversation something which would be of use to her as a guide in future life." One would have thought that this answer would have pleased the queen, but it did not. She did not believe that it was sincere.

On one occasion Mary seriously offended the queen by a remark which she made, and which was, at least, incautious. Kings and queens, and, in fact, all great people in Europe, pride themselves very much upon the antiquity of the line from which they have descended. Now the family of Queen Catharine had risen to rank and distinction within a moderate period; and though she was, as Queen of France, on the very pinnacle of human greatness, she would naturally be vexed at any remark which would remind her of the recentness of her elevation.

# MARY, QUEEN OF SCOTS

Now Mary at one time said, in conversation in the presence of Queen Catharine, that she herself was the descendant of a hundred kings. This was perhaps true, but it brought her into direct comparison with Catharine in a point in which the latter was greatly her inferior, and it vexed and mortified Catharine very much to have such a thing said to her by such a child.

Mary associated thus during all this time, not only with the queen and the princesses, but also with the little prince whom she was destined to marry. His name was Francis, but he was commonly called the *dauphin*, which was the name by which the oldest son of the King of France was then, and has been since designated. The origin of this custom was this. About a hundred years before the time of which we are speaking, a certain nobleman of high rank, who possessed estates in an ancient province of France called Dauphiny, lost his son and heir. He was overwhelmed with affliction at the loss, and finally bequeathed all his estates to the king and his successors, on condition that the oldest son should bear the title of Dauphin. The grant was accepted, and the oldest son was accordingly so styled from that time forward, from generation to generation.

The dauphin, Francis, was a weak and feeble child, but he was amiable and gentle in his manners, and Mary liked him. She met him often in their walks and rides, and she danced with him at the balls and parties given for her amusement. She knew that he was to be her husband as soon as she was old enough to be married, and he knew that she was to be his wife. It was all decided, and nothing which either of them could say or do would have any influence on the result. Neither of them, however, seem to have had any desire to change the result. Mary pitied Francis on account of his feeble health, and liked his amiable and gentle disposition; and Francis could not help loving Mary, both on account of the traits of her character and her personal charms.

As Mary advanced in years, she grew very beautiful. In some of the great processions and ceremonies, the ladies were accustomed to walk, magnificently dressed and carrying torches in their hands. In one of these processions Mary was moving along with the rest, through a crowd of spectators, and the light from her torch fell upon her features and upon her hair in such a manner as to make her appear more beautiful than usual. A woman, standing there, pressed up nearer to her to view her more closely, and, seeing how beautiful she was, asked her if she was not an *angel*. In those days, however, people believed in what is miraculous and supernatural more easily than now, so that it was not very surprising that one should think, in such a case, that an angel from Heaven had come down to join in the procession.

Mary grew up a Catholic, of course: all were Catholics around her. The king and all the royal family were devoted to Catholic observances. The convent, the ceremonies, the daily religious observances enjoined upon her, the splendid churches which she frequented, all tended in their influence to lead her mind away from the Protestant religion which prevailed in her native land, and to make her a Catholic: she remained so throughout her life. There is no doubt that she was conscientious in her attachment to the forms and to the spirit of the Roman Church. At any rate, she was faithful to the ties which her early education imposed upon her, and this fidelity became afterward the source of some of her heaviest calamities and woes.

# 3

## The Great Wedding

### 1558

*Hastening the wedding.—Reasons for it.—Attempt to poison Mary.—The Guises.—Catharine's jealousy.—Commissioners from Scotland.—Preliminaries.—Stipulations.—Plan of Henry to evade them.—Marriage settlement.—Secret papers.—Their contents.—Ceremonies.—The betrothal.—The Louvre.—Notre Dame.—View of the interior.—Amphitheater.—Covered gallery.—The procession.—Mary's dress.—Appearance of Mary.—Wedding ring.—Movement of the procession.—Largess.—Confusion.—The choir.—Mass.—Return of the procession.—Collation.—Ball.—Evening's entertainments.—A tournament.—Rank of the combatants.—Lances.—Rapid evolutions.—Tourner.—Francis's feebleness.—Mary's love for him.—He retires to the country.—Rejoicings in Scotland.—Mons Meg.—Large ball.—Celebration of Mary's marriage.*

WHEN Mary was about fifteen years of age, the King of France began to think that it was time for her to be married. It is true that she was still very young, but there were strong reasons for having the marriage take place at the earliest possible period, for fear that something might occur to prevent its consummation at all. In fact, there were very strong parties opposed to it altogether. The whole Protestant interest in Scotland were opposed to it, and were continually contriving plans to defeat it. They thought that if Mary married a French prince, who was, of course, a Catholic, she would become wedded to the Catholic interest hopelessly and forever. This made them feel a most bitter and determined opposition to the plan.

In fact, so bitter and relentless were the animosities that grew out of this question, that an attempt was actually made to poison Mary. The man who committed this crime was an archer in the king's guard: he was a Scotch man, and his name was Stewart. His attempt was discovered in time to prevent the accomplishment of his purpose. He was tried and condemned. They made every effort to induce him to explain the reason which led him to such an act, or, if he was employed by others, to reveal their names; but he would reveal nothing. He was executed for his crime, leaving mankind to conjecture that his motive, or that of the persons who instigated him to the deed, was a desperate determination to save Scotland, at all hazards, from falling under the influence of papal power.

Mary's mother, the queen dowager of Scotland, was of a celebrated French family, called the family of Guise. She is often, herself, called in history, Mary of Guise. There were other great families in France who were very jealous of the Guises, and envious of their influence and power. They opposed Queen Mary's marriage to the dauphin, and were ready to do all in their power to thwart and defeat it. Queen Catharine, too, who seemed to feel a greater and greater degree of envy and jealousy against Mary as she saw her increasing in grace, beauty, and influence with her advancing years, was supposed to be averse to the marriage. Mary was, in some sense, her rival, and she could not bear to have her become the wife of her son.

King Henry, finding all these opposing influences at work, thought that the safest plan would be to have the marriage carried into effect at the earliest possible period. When, therefore, Mary was about fifteen years of age, which was in 1557, he sent to Scotland, asking the government there to appoint some commissioners to come to France to assent to the marriage contracts, and to witness the ceremonies of the betrothment and the wedding. The marriage contracts, in the case of the union of a queen of one country with a prince of another, are documents of very high importance. It is considered necessary not only to make very formal provision for the personal welfare and comfort of the wife during her married life, and during her widowhood in case of the death of her husband, but also to settle beforehand the questions of succession which might arise out of the marriage, and to define precisely the rights and powers both of the husband and the wife, in the two countries to which they respectively belong.

The Parliament of Scotland appointed a number of commissioners, of the highest rank and station, to proceed to France, and to act there as the representatives of Scotland in every thing which pertained to the marriage. They charged them to guard well the rights and powers of Mary, to see that these rights and all the interests of Scotland were well protected in the marriage contracts, and to secure proper provision for the personal comfort and happiness of the queen. The number of these commissioners was eight. Their departure from Scotland was an event of great public importance. They were accompanied by a large number of attendants and followers, who were eager to be present in Paris at the marriage festivities. The whole company arrived safely at Paris, and were received with every possible mark of distinction and honor.

The marriage contracts were drawn up, and executed with great formality. King Henry made no objection to any of the stipulations and provisions which the commissioners required, for he had a secret plan for evading them all. Very ample provision was made for Mary herself. She was to have a very large income. In case the dauphin died while he was dauphin, leaving Mary a widow, she was still to have a large income paid to her by the French government as long as she lived, whether she remained in France or went back to Scotland. If her husband outlived his father, so as to become King of France, and then died, leaving Mary his widow, her income for the rest of her life was to be double what it would have been if he had died while dauphin. Francis was, in the mean time, to share with her the government of Scotland. If they had a son, he was to be, after their deaths, King of France and of Scotland too. Thus the two crowns would have been united. If, on the other hand, they had only daughters, the oldest one was to be Queen of Scotland only, as the laws of France did not allow a female to inherit the throne. In case they had no children, the crown of Scotland was not to come into the French family at all, but to descend regularly to the next Scotch heir.

Henry was not satisfied with this entirely, for he wanted to secure the union of the Scotch and French crowns at all events, whether Mary had children or not; and he persuaded Mary to sign some papers with him privately, which he thought would secure his purposes, charging her not to let the commissioners know that she had signed them. He thought it possible that he should never have occasion to produce them. One of these papers conveyed the crown of Scotland to the King of France absolutely and forever, in case Mary should die without children. Another provided that the Scotch government should repay him for the enormous sums he had expended upon Mary during her residence in France, for her education, her attendants, the celebrations and galas which he had provided for her, and all the splendid journeys, processions, and parades. His motive in all this expense had been to unite the crown of Scotland to that of France, and he wished to provide that if any thing should occur to prevent the execution of his plan, he could have all this money reimbursed to him again. He estimated the amount at a million of pieces of gold. This was an enormous sum: it shows on how magnificent a scale Mary's reception and entertainment in France were managed.

These preliminary proceedings being settled, all Paris, and, in fact, all France, began to prepare for the marriage celebrations. There were to be two great ceremonies connected with the occasion. The first was the betrothment, the second was the marriage. At the betrothment Francis and Mary were to meet in a great public hall, and there, in the presence of a small and select assemblage of the lords and ladies of the court, and persons of distinction connected with the royal family, they were formally and solemnly to engage themselves to each other. Then,

# MARY, QUEEN OF SCOTS

in about a week afterward, they were to be married, in the most public manner, in the great Cathedral Church of Notre Dame.

The ceremony of the betrothal was celebrated in the palace. The palace then occupied by the royal family was the Louvre. It still stands, but is no longer a royal dwelling. Another palace, more modern in its structure, and called the Tuilleries, has since been built, a little farther from the heart of the city, and in a more pleasant situation. The Louvre is square, with an open court in the center. This open court or area is very large, and is paved like the streets. In fact, two great carriage ways pass through it, crossing each other at right angles in the center, and passing out under great arch-ways in the four sides of the building. There is a large hall within the palace, and in this hall the ceremony of the betrothal took place. Francis and Mary pledged their faith to each other with appropriate ceremonies. Only a select circle of relations and intimate friends were present on this occasion. The ceremony was concluded in the evening with a ball.

In the mean time, all Paris was busy with preparations for the marriage. The Louvre is upon one side of the River Seine, its principal front being toward the river, with a broad street between. There are no buildings, but only a parapet wall on the river side of the street, so that there is a fine view of the river and of the bridges which cross it, from the palace windows. Nearly opposite the Louvre is an island, covered with edifices, and connected, by means of bridges, with either shore. The great church of Notre Dame, where the marriage ceremony was to be performed, is upon this island. It has two enormous square towers in front, which may be seen, rising above all the roofs of the city, at a great distance in every direction. Before the church is a large open area, where vast crowds assemble on any great occasion. The interior of the church impresses the mind with the sublimest emotions. Two rows of enormous columns rise to a great height on either hand, supporting the lofty arches of the roof. The floor is paved with great flat stones, and resounds continually with the footsteps of visitors, who walk to and fro, up and down the aisles, looking at the chapels, the monuments, the sculptures, the paintings, and the antique and grotesque images and carvings. Colored light streams through the stained glass of the enormous windows, and the tones of the organ, and the voices of the priests, chanting the service of the mass, are almost always resounding and echoing from the vaulted roof above.

The words *Notre Dame* mean Our Lady, an expression by which the Roman Catholics denote Mary, the mother of Jesus. The church of Notre Dame had been for many centuries the vast cathedral church of Paris, where all great ceremonies of state were performed. On this occasion they erected a great amphitheater in the area before the church, which would accommodate many thousands of the spectators who were to assemble, and enable them to see the procession. The bride and bridegroom, and their friends, were to assemble in the bishop's palace, which was near the Cathedral, and a covered gallery was erected, leading from this palace to the church, through which the bridal party were to enter. They lined this gallery throughout with purple velvet, and ornamented it in other ways, so as to make the approach to the church through it inconceivably splendid.

Crowds began to collect in the great amphitheater early in the morning. The streets leading to Notre Dame were thronged. Every window in all the lofty buildings around, and every balcony, was full. From ten to twelve the military bands began to arrive, and the long procession was formed, the different parties being dressed in various picturesque costumes. The embassadors of various foreign potentates were present, each bearing their appropriate insignia. The legate of the pope, magnificently dressed, had an attendant bearing before him a cross of massive gold. The bridegroom, Francis the dauphin, followed this legate, and soon afterward came Mary, accompanied by the king. She was dressed in white. Her robe was embroidered with the figure of the lily, and it glittered with diamonds and ornaments of silver. As was the custom in those days, her dress formed a long train, which was borne by two young girls who walked behind her. She wore a diamond necklace, with a ring of immense value suspended from it, and upon her head was a golden coronet, enriched with diamonds and gems of inestimable value.

But the dress and the diamonds which Mary wore were not the chief points of attraction to the spectators. All who were present on the occasion agree in saying that she looked inexpressibly beautiful, and that there was an indescribable grace and charm in all her movements and manner, which filled all who saw her with an intoxication of delight. She was artless and unaffected in her manners, and her countenance, the expression of which was generally placid and calm, was lighted up with the animation and interest of the occasion, so as to make every body envy the dauphin the possession of so beautiful a bride. Queen Catharine, and a long train of the ladies of the court, followed in the procession after Mary. Every body thought that *she* felt envious and ill at ease.

The essential thing in the marriage ceremony was to be the putting of the wedding ring upon Mary's finger, and the pronouncing of the nuptial benediction which was immediately to follow it. This ceremony was to be performed by the Archbishop of Rouen, who was at that time the greatest ecclesiastical dignitary in France. In order that as many persons as possible might witness this, it was arranged that it should be performed at the great door of the church, so as to be in view of the immense throng which had assembled in the amphitheater erected in the area, and of the multitudes which had taken their positions at the windows and balconies, and on the house-tops around. The procession, accordingly, having entered the church through the covered gallery, moved along the aisles and came to the great door. Here a royal pavilion had been erected, where the bridal party could stand in view of the whole assembled multitude. King Henry had the ring. He gave it to the archbishop. The archbishop placed it upon Mary's finger, and pronounced the benediction in a loud voice. The usual congratulations followed, and Mary greeted her husband under the name of his majesty the King of Scotland. Then the whole mighty crowd rent the air with shouts and acclamations.

It was the custom in those days, on such great public occasions as this, to scatter money among the crowd, that they might scramble for it. This was called the king's *largess*; and the largess was pompously proclaimed by heralds before the money was thrown. The throwing of the money among this immense throng produced a scene of indescribable confusion. The people precipitated themselves upon each other in their eagerness to seize the silver and the gold. Some were trampled under foot. Some were stripped of their hats and cloaks, or had their clothes torn from them. Some fainted, and were borne out of the scene with infinite difficulty and danger. At last the people clamorously begged the officers to desist from throwing any more money, for fear that the most serious and fatal consequences might ensue.

In the mean time, the bridal procession returned into the church, and, advancing up the center between the lofty columns, they came to a place called the choir, which is in the heart of the church, and is inclosed by screens of carved and sculptured work. It is in the choir that congregations assemble to be present at mass and other religious ceremonies. Movable seats are placed here on ordinary occasions, but at the time of this wedding the place was fitted up with great splendor. Here mass was performed in the presence of the bridal party. Mass is a solemn ceremony conducted by the priests, in which they renew, or think they renew, the sacrifice of Christ, accompanied with offerings of incense, and other acts of adoration, and the chanting of solemn hymns of praise.

At the close of these services the procession moved again down the church, and, issuing forth at the great entrance, it passed around upon a spacious platform, where it could be seen to advantage by all the spectators. Mary was the center to which all eyes were turned. She moved along, the very picture of grace and beauty, the two young girls who followed her bearing her train. The procession, after completing its circuit, returned to the church, and thence, through the covered gallery, it moved back to the bishop's palace. Here the company partook of a grand collation. After the collation there was a ball, but the ladies were too much embarrassed with their magnificent dresses to be able to dance, and at five o'clock the royal family returned to their home. Mary and Queen Catharine went together in a sort of palanquin, borne by men, high officers of state walking on each side. The king and the dauphin followed on horseback, with a large company in their train; but the streets were every where so crowded with eager spectators that it was with extreme difficulty that they were able to make their way.

The palace to which the party went to spend the evening was fitted up and illuminated in the most splendid manner, and a variety of most curious entertainments had been contrived for the amusement of the company. There were twelve artificial horses, made to move by internal mechanism, and splendidly caparisoned. The children of the company, the little princes and dukes, mounted these horses and rode around the arena. Then came in a company of men dressed like pilgrims, each of whom recited a poem written in honor of the occasion. After this was an exhibition of galleys, or boats, upon a little sea. These boats were large enough to bear up two persons. There were two seats in each, one of which was occupied by a young gentleman. As the boats advanced, one by one, each gentleman leaped to the shore, or to what represented the shore, and, going among the company, selected a lady and bore her off to his boat, and then, seating her in the vacant chair, took his place by her side, and continued his voyage. Francis was in one of the boats, and he, on coming to the shore, took *Mary* for his companion.

The celebrations and festivities of this famous wedding continued for fifteen days. They closed with a grand tournament. A tournament was a very magnificent spectacle in those days. A field was inclosed, in which kings, and princes, and knights, fully armed, and mounted on war-horses, tilted against each other with lances and blunted swords. Ladies of high rank were present as spectators and judges, and one was appointed at each tournament to preside, and to distribute the honors and rewards to those who were most successful in the contests. The greatest possible degree of deference and honor was paid to the ladies by all the knights on these occasions. Once, at a tournament in London, arranged by a king of England, the knights and noblemen rode in a long procession to the field, each led by a lady by means of a silver chain. It was a great honor to be admitted to a share in these contests, as none but persons of the highest rank were allowed to take a part in them. Whenever one was to be held, invitations were sent to all the courts of Europe, and kings, queens, and sovereign princes came to witness the spectacle.

The horsemen who contended on these occasions carried long lances, blunt, indeed, at the end, so that they could not penetrate the armor of the antagonist at which they were aimed, but yet of such weight that the momentum of the blow was sometimes sufficient to unhorse him. The great object of every combatant was, accordingly, to protect himself from this danger. He must turn his horse suddenly, and avoid the lance of his antagonist; or he must strike it with his own, and thus parry the blow; or if he must encounter it, he was to brace himself firmly in his saddle, and resist its impulse with all the strength that he could command. It required, therefore, great strength and great dexterity to excel in a tournament. In fact, the rapidity of the evolutions which it required gave origin to the name, the word tournament being formed from a French word [Touner] which signifies to turn.

The princes and noblemen who were present at the wedding all joined in the tournament except the poor bridegroom, who was too weak and feeble in body, and too timid in mind, for any such rough and warlike exercises. Francis was very plain and unprepossessing in countenance, and shy and awkward in his manners. His health had always been very infirm, and though his rank was very high, as he was the heir apparent to what was then the greatest throne in Europe, every body thought that in all other respects he was unfit to be the husband of such a beautiful and accomplished princess as Mary. He was timid, shy, and anxious and unhappy in disposition. He knew that the gay and warlike spirits around him could not look upon him with respect, and he felt a painful sense of his inferiority.

Mary, however, loved him. It was a love, perhaps, mingled with pity. She did not assume an air of superiority over him, but endeavored to encourage him, to lead him forward, to inspire him with confidence and hope, and to make him feel his own strength and value. She was herself of a sedate and thoughtful character, and with all her intellectual superiority, she was characterized by that feminine gentleness of spirit, that disposition to follow and to yield rather than to govern, that desire to be led and to be loved rather than to lead and be admired, which constitute the highest charm of woman.

Francis was glad when the celebrations, tournament and all, were well over. He set off from Paris with his young bride to one of his country residences, where he could live, for a while, in peace and quietness. Mary was released, in some degree, from the restraints, and formalities, and rules of etiquette of King Henry's court, and was, to some extent, her own mistress, though still surrounded with many attendants, and much parade and splendor. The young couple thus commenced the short period of their married life. They were certainly a very *young* couple, being both of them under sixteen.

The rejoicings on account of the marriage were not confined to Paris. All Scotland celebrated the event with much parade. The Catholic party there were pleased with the final consummation of the event, and all the people, in fact, joined, more or less, in commemorating the marriage of their queen. There is in the Castle of Edinburgh, on a lofty platform which overlooks a broad valley, a monstrous gun, several centuries old, which was formed of bars of iron secured by great iron hoops. The balls which this gun carried are more than a foot in diameter. The name of this enormous piece of ordnance is *Mons Meg*. It is now disabled, having been burst, many years ago, and injured beyond the possibility of repair. There were great rejoicings in Edinburgh at the time of Mary's marriage, and from some old accounts which still remain at the castle, it appears that ten shillings were paid to some men for moving up Mons Meg to the embrasure of the battery, and for finding and bringing back her shot after she was discharged; by which it appears that firing Mons

Meg was a part of the celebration by which the people of Edinburgh honored the marriage of their queen.

# 4

# Misfortunes

### 1559-1561

*Mary's love for Francis.—How to cherish the passion.—Grand tournament.—Henry's pride.—An encounter.—The helmet.—The vizor.—King Henry wounded.—His death.—The mournful marriage.—The dauphin becomes king.—Catharine superseded.—Mary's gentleness.—Coronation of Francis.—Francis's health declines.—Superstition of the people.—Commotions in Scotland.—Sickness of the queen regent.—Death of Mary's mother.—Illness of Francis.—His last moments and death.—Mary a young widow.—Embassadors from Scotland.—Mary's unwillingness to leave France.—Mary in mourning.—She is called the White Queen.—A device.—Mary's employments.—Her beautiful hands.—Melancholy visit.—Mary returns to Paris.—Jealousy.—Queen Elizabeth.—Her character.—Henry VIII.—Elizabeth's claim to the throne.—Mary's claim.—The coat of arms.—Elizabeth offended and alarmed.—The Catholic party.—A device.—Treaty of Edinburgh.—The safe-conduct.—Elizabeth refuses the safe-conduct.—Mary's speech.—Mary's true nobility of soul.—Sympathy with her.—Mary's religious faith.—Her frankness and candor.*

IT was said in the last chapter that Mary loved her husband, infirm and feeble as he was both in body and in mind. This love was probably the effect, quite as much as it was the cause, of the kindness which she showed him. As we are very apt to hate those whom we have injured, so we almost instinctively love those who have in any way become the objects of our kindness and care. If any wife, therefore, wishes for the pleasure of loving her husband, or which is, perhaps, a better supposition, if any husband desires the happiness of loving his wife, conscious that it is a pleasure which he does not now enjoy, let him commence by making her the object of his kind attentions and care, and love will spring up in the heart as a consequence of the kind of action of which it is more commonly the cause.

About a year passed away, when at length another great celebration took place in Paris, to honor the marriages of some other members of King Henry's family. One of them was Francis's oldest sister. A grand tournament was arranged on this occasion too. The place for this tournament was where the great street of St. Antoine now lies, and which may be found on any map of Paris. A very large concourse of kings and nobles from all the courts of Europe were present. King Henry, magnificently dressed, and mounted on a superb war-horse, was a very prominent figure in all the parades of the occasion, though the actual contests and trials of skill which took place were between younger princes and knights, King Henry and the ladies being generally only spectators and judges. He, however, took a part himself on one or two occasions, and received great applause.

At last, at the end of the third day, just as the tournament was to be closed, King Henry was riding around the field, greatly excited with the pride and pleasure which so magnificent a spectacle was calculated to awaken, when he saw two lances still remaining which had not been broken. The idea immediately seized him of making one more exhibition of his own power and dexterity in such contests. He took one of the lances, and, directing a high officer who was riding near him to take the other, he challenged him to a trial of skill. The name of this officer was Montgomery. Montgomery at first declined, being unwilling to contend with his king. The king insisted. Queen Catharine begged that he would not contend again. Accidents sometimes happened, she knew, in these rough encounters; and, at any rate, it terrified her to see her husband exposed to such dangers. The other lords and ladies, and Francis and Queen Mary particularly, joined in these expostulations. But Henry was inflexible. There was no danger, and, smiling at their fears, he commanded Montgomery to arm himself with his lance and take his position.

The spectators looked on in breathless silence. The two horsemen rode toward each other, each pressing his horse forward to his utmost speed, and as they passed, each aimed his lance at the head and breast of the other. It was customary on such occasions to wear a helmet, with a part called a vizor in front, which could be raised on ordinary occasions, or let down in moments of danger like this, to cover and protect the eyes. Of course this part of the armor was weaker than the rest, and it happened that Montgomery's lance struck here—was shivered—and a splinter of it penetrated the vizor and inflicted a wound upon Henry, on the head, just over the eye. Henry's horse went on. The spectators observed that the rider reeled and trembled in his seat. The whole assembly were in consternation. The excitement of pride and pleasure was every where turned into extreme anxiety and alarm.

They flocked about Henry's horse, and helped the king to dismount. He said it was nothing. They took off his helmet, and found large drops of blood issuing from the wound. They bore him to his palace. He had the magnanimity to say that Montgomery must not be blamed for this result, as he was himself responsible for it entirely. He lingered eleven days, and then died. This was in July, 1559.

One of the marriages which this unfortunate tournament had been intended to celebrate, that of Elizabeth, the king's daughter, had already taken place, having been performed a day or two before the king was wounded; and it was decided, after Henry was wounded, that the other must proceed, as there were great reasons of state against any postponement of it. This second marriage was that of Margaret, his sister. The ceremony in her case was performed in a silent and private manner, at night, by torch-light, in the chapel of the palace, while her brother was dying. The services were interrupted by her sobs and tears.

Notwithstanding the mental and bodily feebleness which seemed to characterize the dauphin, Mary's husband, who now, by the death of his father, became King of France, the event of his accession to the throne seemed to awaken his energies, and arouse him to animation and effort. He was sick himself, and in his bed, in a palace called the Tournelles, when some officers of state were ushered into his apartment, and, kneeling before him, saluted him as king. This was the first announcement of his father's death. He sprang from his bed, exclaiming at once that he was well. It is one of the sad consequences of hereditary greatness and power that a son must sometimes rejoice at the death of his father.

It was Francis's duty to repair at once to the royal palace of the Louvre, with Mary, who was now Queen of France as well as of Scotland, to receive the homage of the various estates of the realm. Catharine was, of course, now queen dowager. Mary, the child whom she had so long looked upon with feelings of jealousy and envy was, from this time, to take her place as queen. It was very humiliating to Catharine to assume the position of a second and an inferior in the presence of one whom she had so long been accustomed to direct and to command. She yielded, however, with a good grace, though she seemed dejected and sad. As they were leaving the Tournelles, she stopped to let Mary go before her, saying, "Pass on, madame; it is your turn to take precedence now." Mary went before her, but she stopped in her turn, with a sweetness of disposition so characteristic of her, to let Queen Catharine enter first into the carriage which awaited them at the door.

Francis, though only sixteen, was entitled to assume the government himself. He went to Rheims, a town northeast of Paris, where is an abbey, which is the ancient place of coronation for the kings of France. Here he was crowned. He appointed his ministers, and evinced, in his management and in his measures, more energy and decision than it was supposed he possessed. He himself and Mary were now, together, on the summit of earthly grandeur. They had many political troubles and cares which can not be related here, but Mary's life was comparatively peaceful and happy, the pleasures which she enjoyed being greatly enhanced by the mutual affection which existed between herself and her husband.

Though he was small in stature, and very unprepossessing in appearance and manners, Francis still evinced in his government a considerable degree of good judgment and of energy. His health, however, gradually declined. He spent much of his time in traveling, and was often dejected and depressed. One circumstance made him feel very unhappy. The people of many of the villages through which he passed, being in those days very ignorant and superstitious, got a rumor into circulation that the king's malady was such that he could only be cured by being bathed in the blood of young children. They imagined that he was traveling to obtain such a bath; and, wherever he came, the people fled, mothers eagerly carrying off their children from this impending danger. The king did not understand the *cause* of his being thus shunned. They concealed it from him, knowing that it would give him pain. He knew only the *fact*, and it made him very sad to find himself the object of this mysterious and unaccountable aversion.

In the mean time, while these occurrences had been taking place in France, Mary's mother, the queen dowager of Scotland, had been made queen regent of Scotland after her return from France; but she experienced infinite trouble and difficulty in managing the affairs of the country. The Protestant party became very strong, and took up arms against her government. The English sent them aid. She, on the other hand, with the Catholic interest to support her, defended her power as well as she could, and called for help from France to sustain her. And thus the country which she was so ambitious to govern, was involved by her management in the calamities and sorrows of civil war.

In the midst of this contest she died. During her last sickness she sent for some of the leaders of the Protestant party, and did all that she could to soothe and conciliate their minds. She mourned the calamities and sufferings which the civil war had brought upon the country, and urged the Protestants to do all in their power, after her death, to heal these dissensions and restore peace. She also exhorted them to remember their obligations of loyalty and obedience to their absent queen, and to sustain and strengthen her government by every means in their power. She died, and after her death the war was brought to a close by a treaty of peace, in which the French and English governments joined with the government of Scotland to settle the points in dispute, and immediately afterward the troops of both these nations were withdrawn. The death of the queen regent was supposed to have been caused by the pressure of anxiety which the cares of her government imposed. Her body was carried home to France, and interred in the royal abbey at Rheims.

The death of Mary's mother took place in the summer of 1560. The next December Mary was destined to meet with a much heavier affliction. Her husband, King Francis, in addition to other complaints, had been suffering for some time from pain and disease in the ear. One day, when he was preparing to go out hunting, he was suddenly seized with a fainting fit, and was soon found to be in great danger. He continued some days very ill. He was convinced himself that he could not recover, and began to make arrangements for his approaching end. As he drew near to the close of his life, he was more and more deeply impressed with a sense of Mary's kindness and love. He mourned very much his approaching separation from her. He sent for his mother, Queen Catharine, to come to his bedside, and begged that she would treat Mary kindly, for his sake, after he was gone.

Mary was overwhelmed with grief at the approaching death of her husband. She knew at once what a great change it would make in her condition. She would lose immediately her rank and station. Queen Catharine would again come into power, as queen regent, during the minority of the next heir. All her friends of the family of Guise, would be removed from office, and she herself would become a mere guest and stranger in the land of which she had been the queen. But nothing could arrest the progress of the disease under which her husband was sinking. He died, leaving Mary a disconsolate widow of seventeen.

The historians of those days say that Queen Catharine was much pleased at the death of Francis her son. It restored her to rank and power. Mary was again beneath her, and in some degree subject to her will. All Mary's friends were removed from their high stations, and others, hostile to her family, were put into their places. Mary soon found herself unhappy at court, and she accordingly removed to a castle at a considerable distance from Paris to the west, near the city of Orleans. The people of Scotland wished her to return to her native land. Both the great parties sent embassadors to her to ask her to return, each of them urging her to adopt such measures on her arrival in Scotland as should favor their cause. Queen Catharine, too, who was still jealous of Mary's influence, and of the admiration and love which her beauty and the loveliness of her character inspired, intimated to her that perhaps it would be better for her now to leave France and return to her own land.

Mary was very unwilling to go. She loved France. She knew very little of Scotland. She was very young when she left it, and the few recollections which she had of the country were confined to the lonely island of Inchmahome and the Castle of Stirling. Scotland was in a cold and inhospitable climate, accessible only through stormy and dangerous seas, and it seemed to her that going there was going into exile. Besides, she dreaded to undertake personally to administer a government whose cares and anxieties had been so great as to carry her mother to the grave.

Mary, however, found that it was in vain for her to resist the influences which pressed upon her the necessity of returning to her native land. She wandered about during the spring and summer after her husband's death, spending her time in various palaces and abbeys, and at length she began to prepare for her return to Scotland. The same gentleness and loveliness of character which she had exhibited in her prosperous fortunes, shone still more conspicuously now in her hours of sorrow. Sometimes she appeared in public, in certain ceremonies of state. She was then dressed in mourning—in white—according to the custom in royal families in those days, her dark hair covered by a delicate crape veil. Her beauty, softened and chastened by her sorrows, made a strong impression upon all who saw her.

She appeared so frequently, and attracted so much attention in her white mourning, that she began to be known among the people as the White Queen. Every body wanted to see her. They admired her beauty; they were impressed with the romantic interest of her history; they pitied her sorrows. She mourned her husband's death with deep and unaffected grief. She invented a device and motto for a seal, appropriate to the occasion: it was a figure of the liquorice-tree, every part of which is useless except the root, which, of course, lies beneath the surface of the earth. Underneath was the inscription, in Latin, *My treasure is in the ground*. The expression is much more beautiful in the Latin than can be expressed in any English words. [Dulce meum terra tegit.]

Mary did not, however, give herself up to sullen and idle grief, but employed herself in various studies and pursuits, in order to soothe and solace her grief by useful occupation. She read Latin authors; she studied poetry; she composed. She paid much attention to music, and charmed those who were in her company by the sweet tones of her voice and her skillful performance upon an instrument. The historians even record a description of the fascinating effect produced by the graceful movements of her beautiful hand. Whatever she did or said seemed to carry with it an inexpressible charm.

Before she set out on her return to Scotland she went to pay a visit to her grandmother, the same lady whom her mother had gone to see in her castle, ten years before, on her return to Scotland after her visit to Mary. During this ten years the unhappy mourner had made no change in respect to her symbols of grief. The apartments of her palace were still hung with black. Her countenance wore the same expression of austerity and woe. Her attendants were trained to pay to her every mark of the most profound deference in all their approaches to her. No sounds of gayety or pleasure were to be heard, but a profound stillness and solemnity reigned continually throughout the gloomy mansion.

Not long before the arrangements were completed for Mary's return to Scotland, she revisited Paris, where she was received with great marks of attention and honor. She was now eighteen or nineteen years of age, in the bloom of her beauty, and the monarch of a powerful kingdom, to which she was about to return, and many of the young princes of Europe began to aspire to the honor of her hand. Through these and other influences, she was the object of much attention; while, on the other hand, Queen Catharine, and the party in power at the French court, were envious and jealous of her popularity, and did a great deal to mortify and vex her.

The enemy, however, whom Mary had most to fear, was her cousin, Queen Elizabeth of England. Queen Elizabeth was a maiden lady, now nearly thirty years of age. She was in all respects extremely different from Mary. She was a zealous Protestant, and very suspicious and watchful in respect to Mary, on account of her Catholic connections and faith. She was very plain in person, and unprepossessing in manners. She was, however, intelligent and shrewd, and was governed by calculations and policy in all that she did. The people by whom she was surrounded admired her talents and feared her power, but nobody loved her. She had many good qualities as a monarch, but none considered as a woman.

Elizabeth was somewhat envious of her cousin Mary's beauty, and of her being such an object of interest and affection to all who knew her. But she had a far more serious and permanent cause of alienation from her than personal envy. It was this: Elizabeth's father, King Henry VIII., had, in succession, several wives, and there had been a question raised about the legality of his marriage with Elizabeth's mother. Parliament decided at one time that this marriage was not valid; at another time, subsequently, they decided that it was. This difference in the two decisions was not owing so much to a change of sentiment in the persons who voted, as to a change in the ascendency of the parties by which the decision was controlled. If the marriage were valid, then Elizabeth was entitled to the English crown. If it were not valid, then she was not entitled to it: it belonged to the next heir. Now it happened that Mary

Queen of Scots was the next heir. Her grandmother on the father's side was an English princess, and through her Mary had a just title to the crown, if Queen Elizabeth's title was annulled.

Now, while Mary was in France, during the lifetime of King Henry, Francis's father, he and the members of the family of Guise advanced Mary's claim to the British crown, and denied that of Elizabeth. They made a coat of arms, in which the arms of France, and Scotland, and England were combined, and had it engraved on Mary's silver plate. On one great occasion, they had this symbol displayed conspicuously over the gateway of a town where Mary was making a public entry. The English embassador, who was present, made this, and the other acts of the same kind, known to Elizabeth, and she was greatly incensed at them. She considered Mary as plotting treasonably against her power, and began to contrive plans to circumvent and thwart her.

Portrait of Queen Elizabeth

Nor was Elizabeth wholly unreasonable in this. Mary, though personally a gentle and peaceful woman, yet in her teens, was very formidable to Elizabeth as an opposing claimant of the crown. All the Catholics in France and in Scotland would naturally take Mary's side. Then, besides this, there was a large Catholic party in England, who would be strongly disposed to favor any plan which should give them a Catholic monarch. Elizabeth was, therefore, very justly alarmed at such a claim on the part of her cousin. It threatened not only to expose her to the aggressions of foreign foes, but also to internal commotions and dangers, in her own dominions.

The chief responsibility for bringing forward this claim must rest undoubtedly, not on Mary herself, but on King Henry of France and the other French princes, who first put it forward. Mary, however, herself, was not entirely passive in the affair. She liked to consider herself as entitled to the English crown. She had a device for a seal, a very favorite one with her, which expressed this claim. It contained two crowns, with a motto in Latin below which meant, "*A third awaits me.*" Elizabeth knew all these things, and she held Mary accountable for all the anxiety and alarm which this dangerous claim occasioned her.

At the peace which was made in Scotland between the French and English forces and the Scotch, by the great treaty of Edinburgh which has been already described, it was agreed that Mary should relinquish all claim to the crown of England. This treaty was brought to France for Mary to ratify it, but she declined. Whatever rights she might have to the English crown, she refused to surrender them. Things remained in this state until the time arrived for her return to her native land, and then, fearing that perhaps Elizabeth might do something to intercept her passage, she applied to her for a safe-conduct; that is, a writing authorizing her to pass safely and without hinderance through the English dominions, whether land or sea. Queen Elizabeth returned word through her embassador in Paris, whose name was Throckmorton, that she could not give her any such safe-conduct, because she had refused to ratify the treaty of Edinburgh.

When this answer was communicated to Mary, she felt deeply wounded by it. She sent all the attendants away, that she might express herself to Throckmorton without reserve. She told him that it seemed to her very hard that her cousin was disposed to prevent her return to her native land. As to her claim upon the English crown, she said that advancing it was not her plan, but that of her husband and his father; and that now she could not properly renounce it, whatever its validity might be, till she could have opportunity to return to Scotland and consult with her government there, since it affected not her personally alone, but the public interests of Scotland. "And now," she continued, in substance, "I am sorry that I asked such a favor of her. I have no need to ask it, for I am sure I have a right to return from France to my own country without asking permission of any one. You have often told me that the queen wished to be on friendly terms with me, and that it was your opinion that to be friends would be best for us both. But now I see that she is not of your mind, but is disposed to treat me in an unkind and unfriendly manner, while she knows that I am her equal in rank, though I do not pretend to be her equal in abilities and experience. Well she may do as she pleases. If my preparations were not so far advanced, perhaps I should give up the voyage. But I am resolved to go. I hope the winds will prove favorable, and carry me away from her shores. If they carry me upon them, and I fall into her hands, she may make what disposal of me she will. If I lose my life, I shall esteem it no great loss, for it is now little else than a burden."

How strongly this speech expresses "that mixture of melancholy and dignity, of womanly softness and noble decision, which pervaded her character." There is a sort of gentleness even in her anger, and a certain indescribable womanly charm in the workings of her mind, which cause all who read her story, while they can not but think that Elizabeth was right, to sympathize wholly with Mary.

Throckmorton, at one of his conversations with Mary, took occasion to ask her respecting her religious views, as Elizabeth wished to know how far she was fixed and committed in her attachment to the Catholic faith. Mary said that she was born and had been brought up a Catholic, and that she should remain so as long as she lived. She would not interfere, she said, with her subjects adopting such form of religion as they might prefer, but for herself she should not change. If she should change, she said, she should justly lose the confidence of her people; for, if they saw that she was light and fickle on that subject, they could not rely upon her in respect to any other. She did not profess to be able to argue, herself, the questions of difference, but she was not wholly uninformed in respect to them, as she had often heard the points discussed by learned men, and had found nothing to lead her to change her ground.

It is impossible for any reader, whether Protestant or Catholic, not to admire the frankness and candor, the honest conscientiousness, the courage, and, at the same time, womanly modesty and propriety which characterize this reply.

# 5

## Return to Scotland

### 1561

*Calais.—Artificial piers and breakwaters.—Throckmorton.—Elizabeth's plans.—Throckmorton baffled.—Throckmorton's advice.—Queen Catharine's farewell.—Escort.—Embarkation.—Spectators.—Unfortunate accident.—Mary's farewell to France.—Her deep emotion.—Mary's first night on board.—Her reluctance to leave France.—Fog.—One vessel captured.—Narrow escape.—Mary's Adieu to France.—Attempts to translate it.—Translations of Mary's Adieu to France.—Arrival at Leith.—Palace of Holyrood.—Mary's arrival unexpected.—Mary's reception.—Contrasts.—The cavalcade.—Serenade.—Solitary home.—Favorable impression.—The Lord James.—Mary makes him one of her ministers.—The mass.—Transubstantiation.—Adoration of the host.—Protestant and Catholic worship.—Violence and persecution.—The mass in Mary's chapel.—Scene of excitement.—Lord James.—The reformer, John Knox.—His uncompromising character.—Knox's interview with Mary.—His sternness subdued.—The four Maries.—Queen Elizabeth's insincerity.*

MARY was to sail from the port of Calais. Calais is on the northern coast of France, opposite to Dover in England, these towns being on opposite sides of the Straits of Dover, where the channel between England and France is very narrow. Still, the distance is so great that the land on either side is ordinarily not visible on the other. There is no good natural harbor at Calais, nor, in fact, at any other point on the French coast. The French have had to supply the deficiency by artificial piers and breakwaters. There are several very capacious and excellent harbors on the English side. This may have been one cause, among others, of the great naval superiority which England has attained.

When Queen Elizabeth found that Mary was going to persevere in her intention of returning to her native land, she feared that she might, after her arrival in Scotland, and after getting established in power there, form a scheme for making war upon *her* dominions, and attempt to carry into effect her claim upon the English crown. She wished to prevent this. Would it be prudent to intercept Mary upon her passage? She reflected on this subject with the cautious calculation which formed so striking a part of her character, and felt in doubt. Her taking Mary a prisoner, and confining her a captive in her own land, might incense Queen Catharine, who was now regent of France, and also awaken a general resentment in Scotland, so as to bring upon her the hostility of those two countries, and thus, perhaps, make more mischief than the securing of Mary's person would prevent.

She accordingly, as a previous step, sent to Throckmorton, her embassador in France, directing him to have an interview with Queen Catharine, and ascertain how far she would feel disposed to take Mary's part. Throckmorton did this. Queen Catharine gave no direct reply. She said that both herself and the young king wished well to Elizabeth, and to Mary too, that it was her desire that the two queens might be on good terms with each other; that she was a friend to them both, and should not take a part against either of them.

This was all that Queen Elizabeth could expect, and she formed her plans for intercepting Mary on her passage. She sent to Throckmorton, asking him to find out, if he could, what port Queen Mary was to sail from, and to send her word. She then gave orders to her naval commanders to assemble as many ships as they could, and hold them in readiness to sail into the seas between England and France, for the purpose of *exterminating the pirates*, which she said had lately become very numerous there.

Throckmorton took occasion, in a conversation which he had with Mary soon after this, to inquire from what port she intended to sail; but she did not give him the information. She suspected his motive, and merely said, in reply to his question, that she hoped the wind would prove favorable for carrying her away as far as possible from the English coast, whatever might be the point from which she should take her departure. Throckmorton then endeavored to find out the arrangements of the voyage by other means, but without much success. He wrote to Elizabeth that he thought Mary would sail either from Havre or Calais; that she would go eastward, along the shore of the Continent, by Flanders and Holland, till she had gained a considerable distance from the English coast, and then would sail north along the eastern shores of the German Ocean. He advised that Elizabeth should send spies to Calais and to Havre, and perhaps to other French ports, to watch there, and to let her know whenever they observed any appearances of preparations for Mary's departure.

In the mean time, as the hour for Mary's farewell to Paris and all its scenes of luxury and splendor, drew near, those who had loved her were drawn more closely to her in heart than ever, and those who had been envious and jealous began to relent, and to look upon her with feelings of compassion and of kind regard. Queen Catharine treated her with extreme kindness during the last few days of her stay, and she accompanied her for some distance on her journey, with every manifestation of sincere affection and good will. She stopped, at length, at St. Germain, and there, with many tears, she bade her gentle daughter-in-law a long and last farewell.

Many princes and nobles, especially of the family of Guise, Mary's relatives, accompanied her through the whole journey. They formed quite a long cavalcade, and attracted great attention in all the towns and districts through which they passed. They traveled slowly, but at length arrived at Calais, where they waited nearly a week to complete the arrangements for Mary's embarkation. At length the day arrived for her to set sail. A large concourse of spectators assembled to witness the scene. Four ships had been provided for the transportation of the party and their effects. Two of these were galleys. They were provided with banks of oars, and large crews of rowers, by means of which the vessels could be propelled when the wind failed. The two other vessels were merely vessels of burden, to carry the furniture and other effects of the passengers.

Many of the queen's friends were to accompany her to Scotland. The four Maries were among them. She bade those that were to remain behind farewell, and prepared to embark on board the royal galley. Her heart was very sad. Just at this time, a vessel which was coming in struck against the pier, in consequence of a heavy sea which was rolling in, and of the distraction of the seamen occasioned by Mary's embarkation. The vessel which struck was so injured by the concussion that it filled immediately and sank. Most of the seamen on board were drowned. This accident produced great excitement and confusion. Mary looked upon the scene from the deck of her vessel, which was now slowly moving from the shore. It alarmed her, and impressed her mind with a sad and mournful sense of the dangers of the elements to whose mercy she was now to be committed for many days. "What an unhappy omen is this!" she exclaimed. She then went to the stern of the ship, looked back at the shore, then knelt down, and, covering her face with her hands, sobbed aloud. "Farewell, France!" she exclaimed: "I shall never, never see thee more." Presently, when her emotions for a moment subsided, she would raise her eyes, and take another view of the slowly-receding shore, and then exclaim again, "Farewell, my beloved France! farewell! farewell!"

## JACOB ABBOTT

Mary's Embarkation at Calais

She remained in this position, suffering this anguish, for five hours, when it began to grow dark, and she could no longer see the shore. She then rose, saying that her beloved country was gone from her sight forever. "The darkness, like a thick veil, hides thee from my sight, and I shall see thee no more. So farewell, beloved land! farewell forever!" She left her place at the stern, but she would not leave the deck. She made them bring up a bed, and place it for her there, near the stern. They tried to induce her to go into the cabin, or at least to take some supper; but she would not. She lay down upon her bed. She charged the helmsman to awaken her at the dawn, if the land was in sight when the dawn should appear. She then wept herself to sleep.

During the night the air was calm, and the vessels in which Mary and her company had embarked made such small progress, being worked only by the oars, that the land came into view again with the gray light of the morning. The helmsman awoke Mary, and the sight of the shore renewed her anguish and tears. She said that she *could not* go. She wished that Elizabeth's ships would come in sight, so as to compel her squadron to return. But no English fleet appeared. On the contrary, the breeze freshened. The sailors unfurled the sails, the oars were taken in, and the great crew of oarsmen rested from their toil. The ships began to make their way rapidly through the rippling water. The land soon became a faint, low cloud in the horizon, and in an hour all traces of it entirely disappeared.

The voyage continued for ten days. They saw nothing of Elizabeth's cruisers. It was afterward ascertained, however, that these ships were at one time very near to them, and were only prevented from seeing and taking them by a dense fog, which at that time happened to cover the sea. One of the vessels of burden was seen and taken, and carried to England. It contained, however, only some of Mary's furniture and effects. She herself escaped the danger.

The fog, which was thus Mary's protection at one time, was a source of great difficulty and danger at another; for, when they were drawing near to the place of their landing in Scotland, they were enveloped in a fog so dense that they could scarcely see from one end of the vessel to the other. They stopped the progress of their vessels, and kept continually sounding; and when at length the fog cleared away, they found themselves involved in a labyrinth of rocks and shoals of the most dangerous character. They made their escape at last, and went on safely toward the land. Mary said, however, that she felt, at the time, entirely indifferent as to the result. She was so disconsolate and wretched at having parted forever from all that was dear to her, that it seemed to her that she was equally willing to live or to die.

Mary, who, among her other accomplishments, had a great deal of poetic talent, wrote some lines, called her Farewell to France, which have been celebrated from that day to this. They are as follows:

ADIEU.

Adieu, plaisant pays de France!
O ma patrie,
La plus cherie;
Qui a nourri ma jeune enfance.
Adieu, France! adieu, mes beaux jours!
La nef qui déjoint mes amours,

N'a cy de moi que la moitié;
Une parte te reste; elle est tienne;
Je la fie à ton amitié,
Pour que de l'autre il te souvienne.

Many persons have attempted to translate these lines into English verse; but it is always extremely difficult to translate poetry from one language to another. We give here two of the best of these translations. The reader can judge, by observing how different they are from each other, how different they must both be from their common original.

ADIEU.

Farewell to thee, thou pleasant shore,
The loved, the cherished home to me
Of infant joy, a dream that's o'er,
Farewell, dear France! farewell to thee.

The sail that wafts me bears away
From thee but half my soul alone;
Its fellow half will fondly stay,
And back to thee has faithful flown.

I trust it to thy gentle care;
For all that here remains with me
Lives but to think of all that's there,
To love and to remember thee.

The other translation is as follows:

ADIEU.

Adieu, thou pleasant land of France!
The dearest of all lands to me,

Where life was like a joyful dance,
The joyful dance of infancy.

Farewell my childhood's laughing wiles,
Farewell the joys of youth's bright day,
The bark that takes me from thy smiles,
Bears but my meaner half away.

The best is thine; my changeless heart
Is given, beloved France, to thee;
And let it sometimes, though we part,
Remind thee, with a sigh, of me.

It was on the 19th of August, 1561, that the two galleys arrived at Leith. Leith is a small port on the shore of the Frith of Forth, about two miles from Edinburgh, which is situated somewhat inland. The royal palace, where Mary was to reside, was called the Palace of Holyrood. It was, and is still, a large square building, with an open court in the center, into which there is access for carriages through a large arched passage-way in the center of the principal front of the building. In the rear, but connected with the palace, there was a chapel in Mary's day, though it is now in ruins. The walls still remain, but the roof is gone. The people of Scotland were not expecting Mary so soon. Information was communicated from country to country, in those days, slowly and with great difficulty. Perhaps the time of Mary's departure from France was purposely concealed even from the Scotch, to avoid all possibility that the knowledge of it should get into Elizabeth's possession.

At any rate, the first intelligence which the inhabitants of Edinburgh and the vicinity had of the arrival of their queen, was the approach of the galleys to the shore, and the firing of a royal salute from their guns. The Palace of Holyrood was not ready for Mary's reception, and she had to remain a day at Leith, awaiting the necessary preparations. In the mean time, the whole population began to assemble to welcome her arrival. Military bands were turned out; banners were prepared; civil and military officers in full costume assembled, and bon-fires and illuminations were provided for the evening and night. In a word, Mary's subjects in Scotland did all in their power to do honor to the occasion; but the preparations were so far beneath the pomp and pageantry which she had been accustomed to in France, that she felt the contrast very keenly, and realized, more forcibly than ever, how great was the change which the circumstances of her life were undergoing.

Palace Of Holyrood with Salisbury Crags and Arthur's Seat in the Distance

Horses were prepared for Mary and her large company of attendants, to ride from Leith to Edinburgh. The long cavalcade moved toward evening. The various professions and trades of Edinburgh were drawn up in lines on each side of the road, and thousands upon thousands of other spectators assembled to witness the scene. When she reached the Palace of Holyrood House, a band of music played for a time under her windows, and then the great throng quietly dispersed, leaving Mary to her repose. The adjoining engraving represents the Palace of Holyrood as it now appears. In Mary's day, the northern part only had been built —that is, the part on the left, in the view, where the ivy climbs about the windows—and the range extending back to the royal chapel, the ruins of which are seen in the rear. Mary took up her abode in this dwelling, and was glad to rest from the fatigues and privations of her long voyage; but she found her new home a solitary and gloomy dwelling, compared with the magnificent palaces of the land she had left.

Mary made an extremely favorable impression upon her subjects in Scotland. To please them, she exchanged the white mourning of France, from which she had taken the name of the White Queen, for a black dress, more accordant with the ideas and customs of her native land. This gave her a more sedate and matronly character, and though the expression of her countenance and figure was somewhat changed by it, it was only a change to a new form of extreme and fascinating beauty. Her manners, too, so graceful and easy, and yet so simple and unaffected, charmed all who saw her.

Mary had a half brother in Scotland, whose title was at this time the Lord James. He was afterward named the Earl of Murray, and is commonly known in history under this latter designation. The mother of Lord James was not legally married to Mary's father, and consequently he could not inherit any of his father's rights to the Scottish crown. The Lord James was, however, a man of very high rank and influence, and Mary immediately received him into her service, and made him one of her highest ministers of state. He was now about thirty years of age, prudent, cautious, and wise, of good person and manners, but somewhat reserved and austere.

Lord James had the general direction of affairs on Mary's arrival, and things went on very smoothly for a week; but then, on the first Sunday after the landing, a very serious difficulty threatened to occur. The Catholics have a certain celebration, called the mass, to which they attach a very serious and solemn importance. When our Savior gave the bread and the wine to his disciples at the Last Supper he said of it, "This is my body, broken for you," and "This is my blood, shed for you." The Catholics understand that these words denote that the bread and wine did at that time, and that they do now, whenever the communion service is celebrated by a priest duly authorized, become, by a sort of miraculous transformation, the true body and blood of Christ, and that the priest, in breaking the one and pouring out the other, is really and truly renewing the great sacrifice for sin made by Jesus Christ at his crucifixion. The mass, therefore, in which the bread and the wine are so broken and poured out, becomes, in their view, not a mere service of prayer and praise to God, but a solemn *act* of sacrifice. The spectators, or assistants, as they call them, meaning all who are present on the occasion, stand by, not merely to hear words of adoration, in which they mentally join, as is the case in most Protestant forms of worship, but to witness the *enactment of a deed*, and one of great binding force and validity: a real and true sacrifice of Christ, made anew, as an atonement for their sins. The bread, when consecrated, and as they suppose, transmuted to the body of Christ, is held up to view, or carried in a procession around the church, that all present may bow before it and adore it as really being, though in the form of bread, the wounded and broken body of the Lord.

Of course the celebration of the mass is invested, in the minds of all conscientious Catholics, with the utmost solemnity and importance. They stand silently by, with the deepest feelings of reverence and awe, while the priest offers up for them, anew, the great sacrifice for sin. They regard all Protestant worship, which consists of mere exhortations to duty, hymns and prayers, as lifeless and void. That which is to them the soul, the essence, and substance of the whole, is wanting. On the other hand, the Protestants abhor the sacrifice of the mass as gross superstition. They think that the bread remains simply bread after the benediction as much as before; that for the priests to pretend that in breaking it they renew the sacrifice of Christ, is imposture; and that to bow before it in adoration and homage is the worst idolatry.

Now it happened that during Mary's absence in France, the contest between the Catholics and the Protestants had been going fiercely on, and the result had been the almost complete defeat of the Catholic party, and the establishment of the Protestant interest throughout the realm. A great many deeds of violence accompanied this change. Churches and abbeys were sometimes sacked and destroyed. The images of saints, which the Catholics had put up, were pulled down and broken; and the people were sometimes worked up to phrensy against the principles of the Catholic faith and Catholic observances. They abhorred the mass, and were determined that it should not be introduced again into Scotland.

Queen Mary, knowing this state of things determined, on her arrival in Scotland, not to interfere with her people in the exercise of their religion; but she resolved to remain a Catholic herself, and to continue, for the use of her own household, in the royal chapel at Holyrood, the same Catholic observances to which she had been accustomed in France. She accordingly gave orders that mass should be celebrated in her chapel on the first Sunday after her arrival. She was very willing to abstain from interfering with the religious usages of her subjects, but she was not willing to give up her own.

The friends of the Reformation had a meeting, and resolved that mass should *not* be celebrated. There was, however, no way of preventing it but by intimidation or violence. When Sunday came, crowds began to assemble about the palace and the chapel, and to fill all the avenues leading to them. The Catholic families who were going to attend the service were treated rudely as they passed. The priests they threatened with death. One, who carried a candle which was to be used in the ceremonies, was extremely terrified at their threats and imprecations. The excitement was very great, and would probably have proceeded to violent extremities, had it not been for Lord James's energy and courage. He was a Protestant, but he took his station at the door of the chapel, and, without saying or doing any thing to irritate the crowd without, he kept them at bay, while the service proceeded. It went on to the close, though greatly interrupted by the confusion and uproar. Many of the French people who came with Mary were so terrified by this scene, that they declared they would not stay in such a country, and took the first opportunity of returning to France.

One of the most powerful and influential of the leaders of the Protestant party at this time was the celebrated John Knox. He was a man of great powers of mind and of commanding eloquence; and he had exerted a vast influence in arousing the people of Scotland to a feeling of strong abhorrence of what they considered the abominations of popery. When Queen Mary of England was upon the throne, Knox had written a book against her, and against queens in general, women having, according to his views, no right to govern. Knox was a man of the most stern and uncompromising character, who feared nothing, respected nothing, and submitted to no restraints in the blunt and plain discharge of what he considered his duty. Mary dreaded his influence and power.

Knox had an interview with Mary not long after her arrival, and it is one of the most striking instances of the strange ascendency which Mary's extraordinary beauty and grace, and the pensive charm of her demeanor, exercised over all that came within her influence, that even John Knox, whom nothing else could soften or subdue, found his rough and indomitable energy half forsaking him in the presence of his gentle queen. She expostulated with him. He half apologized. Nothing had ever drawn the least semblance of an apology from him before. He told her that his book was aimed solely against Queen Mary of England, and not against her; that she had no cause to fear its influence; that, in respect to the freedom with which he had advanced his opinions and theories on the subjects of government and religion, she need not be alarmed, for philosophers had always done this in every age, and yet had lived good citizens of the state, whose institutions they had, nevertheless, in some sense theoretically condemned. He told her, moreover, that he had no intention of troubling her reign; that she might be sure of this, since, if he had such a desire, he should have commenced his measures during her absence, and not have postponed them until her position on the throne was strengthened by her return. Thus he tried to soothe her fears, and to justify himself from the suspicion of having designed any injury to such a gentle and helpless queen. The interview was a very extraordinary spectacle. It was that of a lion laying aside his majestic sternness and strength to dispel the fears and quiet the apprehensions of a dove. The interview was, however, after all, painful and distressing to Mary. Some things which the stern reformer felt it his duty to say to her, brought tears into her eyes.

Mary soon became settled in her new home, though many circumstances in her situation were well calculated to disquiet and disturb her. She lived in the palace at Holyrood. The four Maries continued with her for a time, and then two of them were married to nobles of high rank. Queen Elizabeth sent Mary a kind message, congratulating her on her safe arrival in Scotland, and assuring her that the story of her having attempted to intercept her was false. Mary, who had no means of proving Elizabeth's insincerity, sent her back a polite reply.

# 6

# Mary and Lord Darnley

### 1562-1566

*Stormy scenes.—Lord James.—Acts of cruelty.—Mary's energy and decision.—Her popularity.—Story of Chatelard.—His love and infatuation. —Trial of Chatelard.—His execution and last words.—Mary and Elizabeth.—The English succession.—Claim of Lady Lennox.—Lord Darnley. —Offers of marriage.—Duplicity of Elizabeth.—Melville sent as embassador to Elizabeth.—His reception.—Conversation of Melville and Elizabeth.—Dudley, earl of Leicester.—The "long" lad.—Lord Darnley. —Elizabeth's management.—Darnley's visit to Scotland.—Mary's message to Elizabeth.—Elizabeth's duplicity.—Wemys Castle.—Mary's opinion of Darnley.—His interview with her.—The courtship.—Elizabeth in a rage.—Murray's opposition.—Mary hastens the marriage.—A dangerous plot.—Mary's narrow escape.—The marriage.—The mourner and the bride.—Darnley's contemptible character.—Darnley's imperiousness and pride.—Mary's cares.—Rebellion.—Elizabeth's treatment of the rebels.— Mary's generous conduct to Darnley.—The double throne.—Darnley's cruel ingratitude.*

DURING the three or four years which elapsed after Queen Mary's arrival in Scotland, she had to pass through many stormy scenes of anxiety and trouble. The great nobles of the land were continually quarreling, and all parties were earnest and eager in their efforts to get Mary's influence and power on their side. She had a great deal of trouble with the affairs of her brother, the Lord James. He wished to have the earldom of Murray conferred upon him. The castle and estates pertaining to this title were in the north of Scotland, in the neighborhood of Inverness. They were in possession of another family, who refused to give them up. Mary accompanied Lord James to the north with an army, to put him in possession. They took the castle, and hung the governor, who had refused to surrender at their summons. This, and some other acts of this expedition, have since been considered unjust and cruel; but posterity have been divided in opinion on the question how far Mary herself was personally responsible for them.

Mary, at any rate, displayed a great degree of decision and energy in her management of public affairs, and in the personal exploits which she performed. She made excursions from castle to castle, and from town to town, all over Scotland. On these expeditions she traveled on horseback, sometimes with a royal escort, and sometimes at the head of an army of eighteen or twenty thousand men. These royal progresses were made sometimes among the great towns and cities on the eastern coast of Scotland, and also, at other times, among the gloomy and dangerous defiles of the Highlands. Occasionally she would pay visits to the nobles at their castles, to hunt in their parks, to review their Highland retainers, or to join them in celebrations and fêtes, and military parades.

During all this time, her personal influence and ascendency over all who knew her was constantly increasing; and the people of Scotland, notwithstanding the disagreement on the subject of religion, became more and more devoted to their queen. The attachment which those who were in immediate attendance upon her felt to her person and character, was in many cases extreme. In one instance, this attachment led to a very sad result. There was a young Frenchman, named Chatelard, who came in Mary's train from France. He was a scholar and a poet. He began by writing verses in Mary's praise, which Mary read, and seemed to be pleased with. This increased his interest in her, and led him to imagine that he was himself the object of her kind regard. Finally, the love which he felt for her came to be a perfect infatuation. He concealed himself one night in Mary's bed-chamber, armed, as if to resist any attack which the attendants might make upon him. He was discovered by the female attendants, and taken away, and they, for fear of alarming Mary, did not tell her of the circumstance till the next morning.

Mary was very much displeased, or, at least, professed to be so. John Knox thought that this displeasure was only a pretense. She, however, forbid Chatelard to come any more into her sight. A day or two after this, Mary set out on a journey to the north. Chatelard followed. He either believed that Mary really loved him, or else he was led on by that strange and incontrollable infatuation which so often, in such cases, renders even the wisest men utterly reckless and blind to the consequences of what they say or do. He watched his opportunity, and one night, when Mary retired to her bed-room, he followed her directly in. Mary called for help. The attendants came in, and immediately sent for the Earl of Murray, who was in the palace. Chatelard protested that all he wanted was to explain and apologize for his coming into Mary's room before, and to ask her to forgive him. Mary, however, would not listen. She was very much incensed. When Murray came in, she directed him to run his dagger through the man. Murray, however, instead of doing this, had the offender seized and sent to prison. In a few days he was tried, and condemned to be beheaded. The excitement and enthusiasm of his love continued to the last. He stood firm and undaunted on the scaffold, and, just before he laid his head on the block, he turned toward the place where Mary was then lodging, and said, "Farewell! loveliest and most cruel princess that the world contains!"

In the mean time, Mary and Queen Elizabeth continued ostensibly on good terms. They sent embassadors to each other's courts. They communicated letters and messages to each other, and entered into various negotiations respecting the affairs of their respective kingdoms. The truth was, each was afraid of the other, and neither dared to come to an open rupture. Elizabeth was uneasy on account of Mary's claim to her crown, and was very anxious to avoid driving her to extremities, since she knew that, in that case, there would be great danger of her attempting openly to enforce it. Mary, on the other hand, thought that there was more probability of her obtaining the succession to the English crown by keeping peace with Elizabeth than by a quarrel. Elizabeth was not married, and was likely to live and die single. Mary would then be the next heir, without much question. She wished Elizabeth to acknowledge this, and to have the English Parliament enact it. If Elizabeth would take this course, Mary was willing to waive her claims during Elizabeth's life. Elizabeth, however, was not willing to do this decidedly. She wished to reserve the right to herself of marrying if she chose. She also wished to keep Mary dependent upon her as long as she could. Hence, while she would not absolutely refuse to comply with Mary's proposition, she would not really accede to it, but kept the whole matter in suspense by endless procrastination, difficulties, and delays.

I have said that, after Elizabeth, Mary's claim to the British crown was almost unquestioned. There was another lady about as nearly related to the English royal line as Mary. Her name was Margaret Stuart. Her title was Lady Lennox. She had a son named Henry Stuart, whose title was Lord Darnley. It was a question whether Mary or Margaret were best entitled to consider herself the heir to the British crown after Elizabeth. Mary, therefore, had two obstacles in the way of the accomplishment of her wishes to be Queen of England: one was the claim of Elizabeth, who was already in possession of the throne, and the other the claims of Lady Lennox, and, after her, of her son Darnley. There was a plan of disposing of this last difficulty in a very simple manner. It was, to have Mary marry Lord Darnley, and thus unite these two claims. This plan had been proposed, but there had been no decision in respect to it. There was one objection: that Darnley being Mary's cousin, their marriage was forbidden by the laws of the Catholic Church. There was no way of obviating this difficulty but by applying to the pope to grant them a special dispensation.

In the mean time, a great many other plans were formed for Mary's marriage. Several of the princes and potentates of Europe applied for her hand. They were allured somewhat, no doubt, by her youth and beauty, and still more, very probably, by the desire to annex her kingdom to their dominions. Mary, wishing to please Elizabeth, communicated often with her, to ask her advice and counsel in regard to her marriage. Elizabeth's policy was to embarrass and perplex the whole subject by making difficulties in respect to every plan proposed. Finally, she recommended a gentleman of her own court to Mary—Robert Dudley, whom she afterward made Earl of Leicester—one of her special favorites. The position of Dudley, and the circumstances of the case, were such that mankind have generally supposed that Elizabeth did not seriously imagine that such a plan could be adopted, but that she proposed it, as perverse and intriguing people often do, as a means of increasing the difficulty. Such minds often attempt to prevent doing what *can* be done by proposing and urging what they know is impossible.

In the course of these negotiations, Queen Mary once sent Melville, her former page of honor in France, as a special embassador to Queen Elizabeth, to ascertain more perfectly her views. Melville had followed Mary to Scotland, and had entered her service there as a confidential secretary; and as she had great confidence in his prudence and in his fidelity, she thought him the most suitable person to undertake this mission. Melville afterward lived to an advanced age, and in the latter part of his life he wrote a narrative of his various adventures, and recorded, in quaint and ancient language, many of his conversations and interviews with the two queens. His mission to England was of course a very important event in his life, and one of the most curious and entertaining passages in his memoirs is his narrative of his interviews with the English queen. He was, at the time, about thirty-four years of age. Mary was about twenty-two.

Sir James Melville was received with many marks of attention and honor by Queen Elizabeth. His first interview with her was in a garden near the palace. She first asked him about a letter which Mary had recently written to her, and which, she said, had greatly displeased her; and she took out a reply from her pocket, written in very sharp and severe language, though she said she had not sent it because it was not severe enough, and she was going to write another. Melville asked to see the letter from Mary which had given Elizabeth so much offense; and on reading it, he explained it, and disavowed, on Mary's part, any intention to give offense, and thus finally succeeded in appeasing Elizabeth's displeasure, and at length induced her to tear up her angry reply.

Elizabeth then wanted to know what Mary thought of her proposal of Dudley for her husband. Melville told her that she had not given the subject much reflection, but that she was going to appoint two commissioners, and she wished Elizabeth to appoint two others, and then that the four should meet on the borders of the two countries, and consider the whole subject of the marriage. Elizabeth said that she perceived that Mary did not think much of this proposed match. She said, however, that Dudley stood extremely high in *her* regard, that she was going to make him an earl, and that she should marry him herself were it not that she was fully resolved to live and die a single woman. She said she wished very much to have Dudley become Mary's husband both on account of her attachment to him, and also on account of his attachment to her, which she was sure would prevent his allowing her, that is, Elizabeth, to have any trouble out of Mary's claim to her crown as long as she lived.

Elizabeth also asked Melville to wait in Westminster until the day appointed for making Dudley an earl. This was done, a short time afterward, with great ceremony. Lord Darnley, then a very tall and slender youth of about nineteen, was present on the occasion. His father and mother had been banished from Scotland, on account of some political offenses, twenty years before, and he had thus himself been brought up in England. As he was a near relative of the queen, and a sort of heir-presumptive to the crown, he had a high position at the court, and his office was, on this occasion, to bear the sword of honor before the queen. Dudley kneeled before Elizabeth while she put upon him the badges of his new dignity. Afterward she asked Melville what he thought of him. Melville was polite enough to speak warmly in his favor. "And yet," said the queen, "I suppose you prefer yonder *long* lad," pointing to Darnley. She knew something of Mary's half-formed design of making Darnley her husband. Melville, who did not wish her to suppose that Mary had any serious intention of choosing Darnley, said that "no woman of spirit would choose such a person as he was, for he was handsome, beardless, and lady-faced; in fact, he looked more like a woman than a man."

Melville was not very honest in this, for he had secret instructions at this very time to apply to Lady Lennox, Darnley's mother, to send her son into Scotland, in order that Mary might see him, and be assisted to decide the question of becoming his wife, by ascertaining how she was going to like him personally. Queen Elizabeth, in the mean time, pressed upon Melville the importance of Mary's deciding soon in favor of the marriage with Leicester. As to declaring in favor of Mary's right to inherit the crown after her, she said the question was in the hands of the great lawyers and commissioners to whom she had referred it, and that she heartily wished that they might come to a conclusion in favor of Mary's claim. She should urge the business forward as fast as she could; but the result would depend very much upon the disposition which Mary showed to comply with her wishes in respect to the marriage. She said she should never marry herself unless she was compelled to it on account of Mary's giving her trouble by her claims upon the crown, and forcing her to desire that it should go to her direct descendants. If Mary would act wisely, and as she ought, and follow *her* counsel, she would, in due time, have all her desire.

Some time more elapsed in negotiations and delays. There was a good deal of trouble in getting leave for Darnley to go to Scotland. From his position, and from the state of the laws and customs of the two realms, he could not go without Elizabeth's permission. Finally, Mary sent word to Elizabeth that she would marry Leicester according to her wish, if she would have her claim to the English crown, *after* Elizabeth, acknowledged and established by the English government, so as to have that question definitely and finally settled. Elizabeth sent back for answer to this proposal, that if Mary married Leicester, she would advance him to great honors and dignities, but that she could not do any thing at present about the succession. She also, at the same time, gave permission to Darnley to go to Scotland.

It is thought that Elizabeth never seriously intended that Mary should marry Leicester, and that she did not suppose Mary herself would consent to it on any terms. Accordingly, when she found Mary was acceding to the plan, she wanted to retreat from it herself, and hoped that Darnley's going to Scotland, and appearing there as a new competitor in the field, would tend to complicate and embarrass the question in Mary's mind, and help to prevent the Leicester negotiation from going any further. At any rate, Lord Darnley—then a very tall and handsome young man of nineteen—obtained suddenly permission to go to Scotland. Mary went to Wemys Castle, and made arrangements to have Darnley come and visit her there.

Wemy's Castle. The Scene of Mary's First Interview with Darnley.

Wemys Castle is situated in a most romantic and beautiful spot on the sea-shore, on the northern side of the Frith of Forth. Edinburgh is upon the southern side of the Frith, and is in full view from the windows of the castle, with Salisbury Crags and Arthur's Seat on the left of the city. Wemys Castle was, at this time, the residence of Murray, Mary's brother. Mary's visit to it was an event which attracted a great deal of attention. The people flocked into the neighborhood and provisions and accommodations of every kind rose enormously in price. Every one was eager to get a glimpse of the beautiful queen. Besides, they knew that Lord Darnley was expected, and the rumor that he was seriously thought of as her future husband had been widely circulated, and had awakened, of course, a universal desire to see him.

Mary was very much pleased with Darnley. She told Melville, after their first interview, that he was the handsomest and best proportioned "long man" she had ever seen. Darnley was, in fact, very tall, and as he was straight and slender, he appeared even taller than he really was. He was, however, though young, very easy and graceful in his manners, and highly accomplished. Mary was very much pleased with him. She had almost decided to make him her husband before she saw him, merely from political considerations, on account of her wish to combine his claim with hers in respect to the English crown. Elizabeth's final answer, refusing the terms on which Mary had consented to marry Leicester, which came about this time, vexed her, and determined her to abandon that plan. And now, just in such a crisis, to find Darnley possessed of such strong personal attractions, seemed to decide the question. In a few days her imagination was full of pictures of joy and pleasure, in anticipations of union with such a husband.

The thing took the usual course of such affairs. Darnley asked Mary to be his wife. She said no, and was offended with him for asking it. He offered her a present of a ring. She refused to accept it. But the no meant yes, and the rejection of the ring was only the prelude to the acceptance of something far more important, of which a ring is the symbol. Mary's first interview with Darnley was in February. In April,

## MARY, QUEEN OF SCOTS

Queen Elizabeth's embassador sent her word that he was satisfied that Mary's marriage with Darnley was all arranged and settled.

Queen Elizabeth was, or pretended to be, in a great rage. She sent the most urgent remonstrances to Mary against the execution of the plan. She forwarded, also, very decisive orders to Darnley, and to the Earl of Lennox his father, to return immediately to England. Lennox replied that he could not return, for "he did not think the climate would agree with him!" Darnley sent back word that he had entered the service of the Queen of Scots, and henceforth should obey her orders alone. Elizabeth, however, was not the only one who opposed this marriage. The Earl of Murray, Mary's brother, who had been thus far the great manager of the government under Mary, took at once a most decided stand against it. He enlisted a great number of Protestant nobles with him, and they held deliberations, in which they formed plans for resisting it by force. But Mary, who, with all her gentleness and loveliness of spirit, had, like other women, some decision and energy when an object in which the heart is concerned is at stake, had made up her mind. She sent to France to get the consent of her friends there. She dispatched a commissioner to Rome to obtain the pope's dispensation; she obtained the sanction of her own Parliament; and, in fact, in every way hastened the preparations for the marriage.

Murray, on the other hand, and his confederate lords, were determined to prevent it. They formed a plan to rise in rebellion against Mary, to waylay and seize her, to imprison her, and to send Darnley and his father to England, having made arrangements with Elizabeth's ministers to receive them at the borders. The plan was all well matured, and would probably have been carried into effect, had not Mary, in some way or other, obtained information of the design. She was then at Stirling, and they were to waylay her on the usual route to Edinburgh. She made a sudden journey, at an unexpected time, and by a new and unusual road, and thus evaded her enemies. The violence of this opposition only stimulated her determination to carry the marriage into effect without delay. Her escape from her rebellious nobles took place in June, and she was married in July. This was six months after her first interview with Darnley. The ceremony was performed in the royal chapel at Holyrood. They show, to this day, the place where she is said to have stood, in the now roofless interior.

Mary was conducted into the chapel by Lennox and another nobleman, in the midst of a large company of lords and ladies of the court, and of strangers of distinction, who had come to Edinburgh to witness the ceremony. A vast throng had collected also around the palace. Mary was led to the altar, and then Lord Darnley was conducted in. The marriage ceremony was performed according to the Catholic ritual. Three rings, one of them a diamond ring of great value, were put upon her finger. After the ceremony, largess was proclaimed, and money distributed among the crowd, as had been done in Paris at Mary's former marriage, five years before. Mary then remained to attend the celebration of mass, Darnley, who was not a Catholic, retiring. After the mass, Mary returned to the palace, and changed the mourning dress which she had continued to wear from the time of her first husband's death to that hour, for one more becoming a bride. The evening was spent in festivities of every kind.

We have said that Darnley was personally attractive in respect both to his countenance and his manners; and, unfortunately, this is all that can be said in his favor. He was weak-minded, and yet self-conceited and vain. The sudden elevation which his marriage with a queen gave him, made him proud, and he soon began to treat all around him in a very haughty and imperious manner. He seems to have been entirely unaccustomed to exercise any self-command, or to submit to any restraints in the gratification of his passions. Mary paid him a great many attentions, and took great pleasure in conferring upon him, as her queenly power enabled her to do, distinctions and honors; but, instead of being grateful for them, he received them as matters of course, and was continually demanding more. There was one title which he wanted, and which, for some good reason, it was necessary to postpone conferring upon him. A nobleman came to him one day and informed him of the necessity

# MARY, QUEEN OF SCOTS

of this delay. He broke into a fit of passion, drew his dagger, rushed toward the nobleman, and attempted to stab him. He commenced his imperious and haughty course of procedure even before his marriage, and continued it afterward, growing more and more violent as his ambition increased with an increase of power. Mary felt these cruel acts of selfishness and pride very keenly, but, womanlike, she palliated and excused them, and loved him still.

She had, however, other trials and cares pressing upon her immediately. Murray and his confederates organized a formal and open rebellion. Mary raised an army and took the field against them. The country generally took her side. A terrible and somewhat protracted civil war ensued, but the rebels were finally defeated and driven out of the country. They went to England and claimed Elizabeth's protection, saying that she had incited them to the revolt, and promised them her aid. Elizabeth told them that it would not do for her to be supposed to have abetted a rebellion in her cousin Mary's dominions, and that, unless they would, in the presence of the foreign embassadors at her court, disavow her having done so, she could not help them or countenance them in any way. The miserable men, being reduced to a hard extremity, made this disavowal. Elizabeth then said to them, "Now you have told the truth. Neither I, nor any one else in my name, incited you against your queen; and your abominable treason *may* set an example to my own subjects to rebel against me. So get you gone out of my presence, miserable traitors as you are."

Thus Mary triumphed over all the obstacles to her marriage with the man she loved; but, alas! before the triumph was fully accomplished, the love was gone. Darnley was selfish, unfeeling, and incapable of requiting affection like Mary's. He treated her with the most heartless indifference, though she had done every thing to awaken his gratitude and win his love. She bestowed upon him every honor which it was in her power to grant. She gave him the title of king. She admitted him to share with her the powers and prerogatives of the crown. There is to this day, in Mary's apartments at Holyrood House, a double throne which she had made for herself and her husband, with their initials worked together in the embroidered covering, and each seat surmounted by a crown. Mankind have always felt a strong sentiment of indignation at the ingratitude which could requite such love with such selfishness and cruelty.

# 7

# Rizzio

### 1561-1566

*David Rizzio.—Embassadors.—Rizzio's position.—Rizzio French secretary.—Displeasure of the Scotch nobles.—They treat Rizzio with scorn and contempt.—He consults Melville.—Melville's counsel.—Melville and the queen.—Rizzio's religion.—His services to Mary.—Rizzio's power and influence.—His intimacy with Mary.—Rizzio's exertion in favor of the marriage.—Rizzio and Darnley.—Darnley greatly disliked.—His unreasonable wishes.—The crown matrimonial.—Darnley's ambition.—Darnley's brutality.—Signatures.—Coins.—Rizzio sides with Mary.—Darnley and Ruthven.—A combination.—The secretary and his queen.—Nature of Mary's attachment.—Plot to assassinate Rizzio.—Plan of Holyrood House.—Description.—Apartments.—Morton and Ruthven.—Mary at supper.—Arrangement of the conspirators.—The little upper room.—Murder of Rizzio.—Conversation.—Violence of the conspirators.—Mary a prisoner.—Darnley's usurpation.—Melville.—Mary appeals to the provost.—Mary defeats the conspirators.—Birth of her son.*

MARY had a secretary named David Rizzio. He was from Savoy, a country among the Alps. It was the custom then, as it is now, for the various governments of Europe to have embassadors at the courts of other governments, to attend to any negotiations, or to the transaction of any other business which might arise between their respective sovereigns. These embassadors generally traveled with pomp and parade, taking sometimes many attendants with them. The embassador from Savoy happened to bring with him to Scotland, in his train, this young man, Rizzio, in 1561, that is, just about the time that Mary herself returned to Scotland. He was a handsome and agreeable young man, but his rank and position were such that, for some years, he attracted no attention.

He was, however, quite a singer, and they used to bring him in sometimes to sing in Mary's presence with three other singers. His voice, being a good bass, made up the quartette. Mary saw him in this way, and as he was a good French and Italian scholar, and was amiable and intelligent, she gradually became somewhat interested in him. Mary had, at this time, among her other officers, a French secretary, who wrote for her, and transacted such other business as required a knowledge of the French language. This French secretary went home, and Mary appointed Rizzio to take his place.

The native Scotchmen in Mary's court were naturally very jealous of the influence of these foreigners. They looked down with special contempt on Rizzio, considering him of mean rank and position, and wholly destitute of all claim to the office of confidential secretary to the queen. Rizzio increased the difficulty by not acting with the reserve and prudence which his delicate situation required. The nobles, proud of their own rank and importance, were very much displeased at the degree of intimacy and confidence to which Mary admitted him. They called him an intruder and an upstart. When they came in and found him in conversation with the queen, or whenever he accosted her freely, as he was wont to do, in their presence, they were irritated and vexed. They did not dare to remonstrate with Mary, but they took care to express their feelings of resentment and scorn to the subject of them in every possible way. They scowled upon him. They directed to him looks of contempt. They turned their backs upon him, and jostled him in a rude and insulting manner. All this was a year or two before Mary's marriage.

Rizzio consulted Melville, asking his judgment as to what he had better do. He said that, being Mary's French secretary, he was necessarily a good deal in her company, and the nobles seemed displeased with it; but he did not see what he could do to diminish or avoid the difficulty. Melville replied that the nobles had an opinion that he not only performed the duties of French secretary, but that he was fast acquiring a great ascendency in respect to all other affairs. Melville further advised him to be much more cautious in his bearing than he had been, to give place to the nobles when they were with him in the presence of the queen, to speak less freely, and in a more unassuming manner, and to explain the whole case to the queen herself, that she might co-operate with him in pursuing a course which would soothe and conciliate the irritated and angry feelings of the nobles. Melville said, moreover, that he had himself, at one time, at a court on the Continent, been placed in a very similar situation to Rizzio's, and had been involved in the same difficulties, but had escaped the dangers which threatened him by pursuing himself the course which he now recommended.

Rizzio seemed to approve of this counsel, and promised to follow it; but he afterward told Melville that he had spoken to the queen on the subject, and that she would not consent to any change, but wished every thing to go on as it had done. Now the queen, having great confidence in Melville, had previously requested him, that if he saw any thing in her deportment, or management, or measures, which he thought was wrong, frankly to let her know it, that she might be warned in season, and amend. He thought that this was an occasion which required this friendly interposition, and he took an opportunity to converse with her on the subject in a frank and plain, but still very respectful manner. He made but little impression. Mary said that Rizzio was only her private French secretary; that he had nothing to do with the affairs of the government; that, consequently, his appointment and his office were her own private concern alone, and she should continue to act according to her own pleasure in managing her own affairs, no matter who was displeased by it.

It is probable that the real ground of offense which the nobles had against Rizzio was jealousy of his superior influence with the queen. They, however, made his religion a great ground of complaint against him. He was a Catholic, and had come from a strong Catholic country, having been born in the northern part of Italy. The Italian language was his mother tongue. They professed to believe that he was a secret emissary of the pope, and was plotting with Mary to bring Scotland back under the papal dominion.

In the mean time, Rizzio devoted himself with untiring zeal and fidelity to the service of the queen. He was indefatigable in his efforts to please her, and he made himself extremely useful to her in a thousand different ways. In fact, his being the object of so much dislike and aversion on the part of others, made him more and more exclusively devoted to the queen, who seemed to be almost his only friend. She, too, was urged, by what she considered the unreasonable and bitter hostility of which her favorite was the object, to bestow upon him greater and greater favors. In process of time, one after another of those about the court, finding that Rizzio's influence and power were great and were increasing, began to treat him with respect, and to ask for his assistance in gaining their ends. Thus Rizzio found his position becoming stronger, and the probability began to increase that he would at length triumph over the enemies who had set their faces so strongly against him.

Though he had been at first inclined to follow Melville's advice, yet he afterward fell in cordially with the policy of the queen, which was, to press boldly forward, and put down with a strong hand the hostility which had been excited against him. Instead, therefore, of attempting to conceal the degree of favor which he enjoyed with the queen, he boasted of and displayed it. He would converse often and familiarly with her in public. He dressed magnificently, like persons of the highest rank, and had many attendants. In a word, he assumed all the airs and manners of a person of high distinction and commanding influence. The external signs of hostility to him were thus put down, but the fires of hatred burned none the less fiercely below, and only wanted an opportunity to burst into an explosion.

Things were in this state at the time of the negotiations in respect to Darnley's marriage; for, in order to take up the story of Rizzio from the beginning, we have been obliged to go back in our narrative. Rizzio exerted all his influence in favor of the marriage, and thus both strengthened his influence with Mary and made Darnley his friend. He did all in his power to diminish the opposition to it, from whatever quarter it might come, and rendered essential service in the correspondence with France, and in the negotiations with the pope for obtaining the necessary dispensation. In a word, he did a great deal to promote the marriage, and to facilitate all the arrangements for carrying it into effect.

Darnley relied, therefore, upon Rizzio's friendship and devotion to his service, forgetting that, in all these past efforts, Rizzio was acting out of regard to Mary's wishes, and not to his own. As long, therefore, as Mary and Darnley continued to pursue the same objects and aims, Rizzio was the common friend and ally of both. The enemies of the marriage, however, disliked Rizzio more than ever.

As Darnley's character developed itself gradually after his marriage, every body began to dislike him also. He was unprincipled and vicious, as well as imperious and proud. His friendship for Rizzio was another ground of dislike to him. The ancient nobles, who had been accustomed to exercise the whole control in the public affairs of Scotland, found themselves supplanted by this young Italian singer, and an English boy not yet out of his teens. They were exasperated beyond all bounds, but yet they contrived, for a while, to conceal and dissemble their anger.

It was not very long after the marriage of Mary and Darnley before they began to become alienated from each other. Mary did every thing for her husband which it was reasonable for him to expect her to do. She did, in fact, all that was in her power. But he was not satisfied. She made him the sharer of her throne. He wanted her to give up *her* place to him, and thus make him the sole possessor of it. He wanted what was called the *crown matrimonial*. The *crown matrimonial* denoted power with which, according to the old Scottish law, the husband of a queen could be invested, enabling him to exercise the royal prerogative in his own name, both during the life of the queen and also after her death, during the continuance of his own life. This made him, in fact, a king for life, exalting him above his wife, the real sovereign, through whom alone he derived his powers.

Now Darnley was very urgent to have the crown matrimonial conferred upon him. He insisted upon it. He would not submit to any delay. Mary told him that this was something entirely beyond her power to grant. The crown matrimonial could only be bestowed by a solemn enactment of the Scottish Parliament. But Darnley, impatient and reckless, like a boy as he was, would not listen to any excuse, but teased and tormented Mary about the crown matrimonial continually.

Besides the legal difficulties in the way of Mary's conferring these powers upon Darnley by her own act, there were other difficulties, doubtless, in her mind, arising from the character of Darnley, and his unfitness, which was every day becoming more manifest, to be intrusted with such power. Only four months after his marriage, his rough and cruel treatment of Mary became intolerable. One day, at a house in Edinburgh, where the king and queen, and other persons of distinction had been invited to a banquet, Darnley, as was his custom, was beginning to drink very freely, and was trying to urge other persons there to drink to excess. Mary expostulated with him, endeavoring to dissuade him from such a course. Darnley resented these kind cautions, and retorted upon her in so violent and brutal a manner as to cause her to leave the room and the company in tears.

When they were first married, Mary had caused her husband to be proclaimed king, and had taken some other similar steps to invest him with a share of her own power. But she soon found that in doing this she had gone to the extreme of propriety, and that, for the future, she must retreat rather than advance. Accordingly, although he was associated with her in the supreme power, she thought it best to keep precedence for her own *name* before his, in the exercise of power. On the coins which were struck, the inscription was, "In the name of the *Queen* and *King* of Scotland." In signing public documents, she insisted on having her name recorded first. These things irritated and provoked Darnley more and more. He was not contented to be admitted to a share of the sovereign power which the queen possessed in her own right alone. He wished to supplant her in it entirely.

Rizzio, of course, took Queen Mary's part in these questions. He opposed the grant of the crown matrimonial. He opposed all other plans for increasing or extending in any way Darnley's power. Darnley was very much incensed against him, and earnestly desired to find some way to effect his destruction. He communicated these feelings to a certain fierce and fearless nobleman named Ruthven, and asked his assistance to contrive some way to take vengeance upon Rizzio.

Ruthven was very much pleased to hear this. He belonged to a party of the lords of the court who also hated Rizzio, though they had hated Darnley besides so much that they had not communicated to him their hostility to the other. Ruthven and his friends had not joined Murray and the other rebels in opposing the marriage of Darnley. They had chosen to acquiesce in it, hoping to maintain an ascendency over Darnley, regarding him, as they did, as a mere boy, and thus retain their power. When they found, however, that he was so headstrong and unmanageable, and that they could do nothing with him, they exerted all their influence to have Murray and the other exiled lords pardoned and allowed to return, hoping to combine with them after their return, and then together to make their power superior to that of Darnley and Rizzio. They considered Darnley and Rizzio both as their rivals and enemies. When they found, therefore, that Darnley was plotting Rizzio's destruction, they felt a very strong as well as a very unexpected pleasure.

Thus, among all the jealousies, and rivalries, and bitter animosities of which the court was at this time the scene, the only true and honest attachment of one heart to another seems to have been that of Mary to Rizzio. The secretary was faithful and devoted to the queen, and the queen was grateful and kind to the secretary. There has been some question whether this attachment was an innocent or a guilty one. A painting, still hanging in the private rooms which belonged to Mary in the palace at Holyrood, represents Rizzio as young and very handsome; on the other hand, some of the historians of the day, to disprove the possibility of any guilty attachment, say that he was rather old and ugly. We may ourselves, perhaps, safely infer, that unless there were something specially repulsive in his appearance and manner, such a heart as Mary's, repelled so roughly from the one whom it was her duty to love, could not well have resisted the temptation to seek a retreat and a refuge in the kind devotedness of such a friend as Rizzio proved himself to be to her.

However this may be, Ruthven made such suggestions to Darnley as goaded him to madness, and a scheme was soon formed for putting Rizzio to death. The plan, after being deliberately matured in all its arrangements, was carried into effect in the following manner. The event occurred early in the spring of 1566, less than a year after Mary's marriage.

Morton, who was one of the accomplices, assembled a large force of his followers, consisting, it is said, of five hundred men, which he posted in the evening near the palace, and when it was dark he moved them silently into the central court of the palace, through the entrance *E*, as marked upon the following plan.

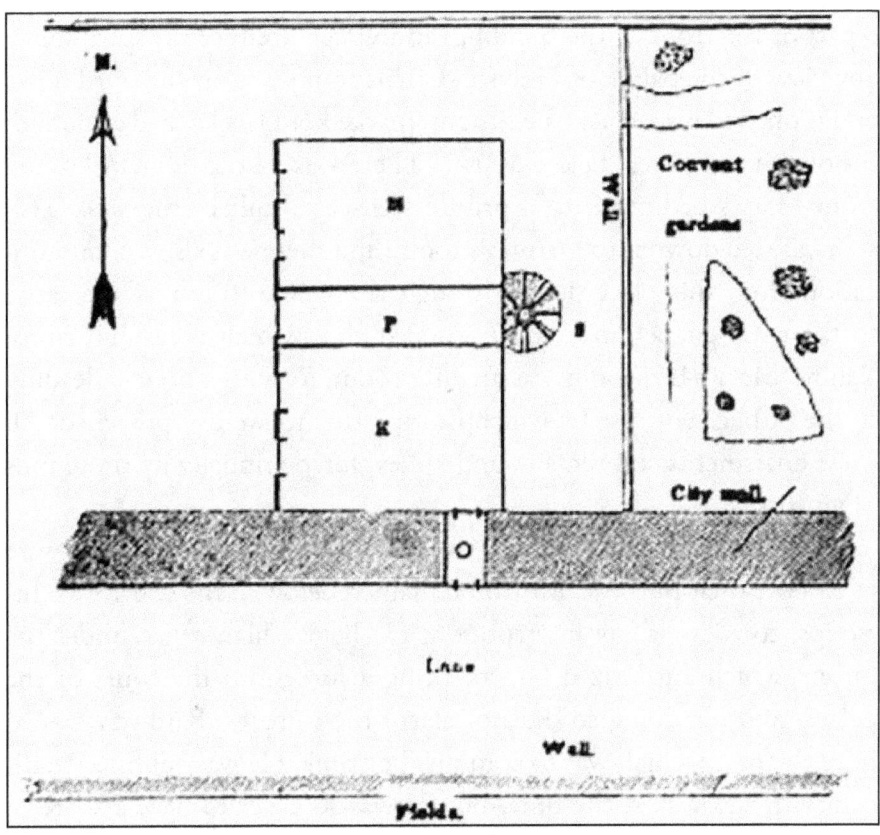

Plan of that part of Holyrood House which was the scene of Rizzio's murder

E. Principal entrance. Co. Court of the palace. PP. Piazza around it. AA. Various apartments built in modern times. H. Great hall, used now as a gallery of portraits. T. Stair-case. o. Entrance to Mary's apartments, second floor. R. Ante-room. B. Mary's bed-room. D. Dressing-room in one of the towers. C. Cabinet, or small room in the other tower. SS. Stair-cases in the wall. d. Small entrance under the tapestry. Ch. Royal chapel. m. Place where Mary and Darnley stood at the marriage ceremony. Pa. Passage-way leading to the chapel.

Mary was, at the time of these occurrences in the little room marked *C*, which was built within one of the round towers which form a part of the front of the building, and which are very conspicuous in any view of the palace of Holyrood. This room was on the third floor, and it opened into Mary's bed-room, marked *B*. Darnley had a room of his own immediately below Mary's. There was a little door, *d*, leading from Mary's bed-room to a private stair-case built in the wall. This stair-case led down into Darnley's room; and there was also a communication from this place down through the whole length of the castle to the royal chapel, marked *Ch*, the building which is now in ruins. Behind Mary's bed-room was an ante-room, *R*, with a door, *o*, leading to the public stair-case by which her apartments were approached. All these apartments still remain, and are explored annually by thousands of visitors.

It was about seven o'clock in the evening that the conspirators were to execute their purpose. Morton remained below in the court with his troops, to prevent any interruption. He held a high office under the queen, which authorized him to bring a force into the court of the palace, and his doing so did not alarm the inmates. Ruthven was to head the party which was to commit the crime. He was confined to his bed with sickness at the time, but he was so eager to have a share in the pleasure of destroying Rizzio, that he left his bed, put on a suit of armor, and came forth to the work. The armor is preserved in the little apartment which was the scene of the tragedy to this day.

Mary was at supper. Two near relatives and friends of hers—a gentleman and a lady—and Rizzio, were with her. The room is scarcely large enough to contain a greater number. There were, however, two or three servants in attendance at a side-table. Darnley came up, about eight o'clock, to make observations. The other conspirators were concealed in his room below, and it was agreed that if Darnley found any cause for not proceeding with the plan, he was to return immediately and give them notice. If, therefore, he should not return, after the lapse of a reasonable time, they were to follow him up the private stair-case, prepared to act at once and decidedly as soon as they should enter the room. They were to come up by this private stair-case, in order to avoid being intercepted or delayed by the domestics in attendance in the ante-room, *R*, of which there would have been danger if they had ascended by the public stair-case at *T*.

Finding that Darnley did not return, Ruthven with his party ascended the stairs, entered the bed-chamber through the little door at *d*, and thence advanced to the door of the cabinet, his heavy iron armor clanking as he came. The queen, alarmed, demanded the meaning of this intrusion. Ruthven, whose countenance was grim and ghastly from the conjoined influence of ferocious passion and disease, said that they meant no harm to her, but they only wanted the villain who stood near her. Rizzio perceived that his hour was come. The attendants flocked in to the assistance of the queen and Rizzio. Ruthven's confederates advanced to join in the attack, and there ensued one of those scenes of confusion and terror, of which those who witness it have no distinct recollection on looking back upon it when it is over. Rizzio cried out in an agony of fear, and sought refuge behind the queen; the queen herself fainted; the table was overturned; and Rizzio, having received one wound from a dagger, was seized and dragged out through the bed-chamber, *B*, and through the ante-room, *R*, to the door, *o*, where he fell down, and was stabbed by the murderers again and again, till he ceased to breathe.

After this scene was over, Darnley and Ruthven came coolly back into Mary's chamber, and, as soon as Mary recovered her senses, began to talk of and to justify their act of violence, without, however, telling her that Rizzio had been killed. Mary was filled with emotions of resentment and grief. She bitterly reproached Darnley for such an act of cruelty as breaking into her apartment with armed men, and seizing and carrying off her friend. She told him that she had raised him from his comparatively humble position to make him her husband, and now this was his return. Darnley replied that Rizzio had supplanted him in her confidence, and thwarted all his plans, and that Mary had shown herself utterly regardless of his wishes, under the influence of Rizzio. He said that, since Mary had made herself his wife, she ought to have obeyed him, and not put herself in such a way under the direction of another. Mary learned Rizzio's fate the next day.

The violence of the conspirators did not stop with the destruction of Rizzio. Some of Mary's high officers of government, who were in the palace at the time, were obliged to make their escape from the windows to avoid being seized by Morton and his soldiers in the court. Among them was the Earl Bothwell, who tried at first to drive Morton out, but in the end was obliged himself to flee. Some of these men let themselves down by ropes from the outer windows. When the uproar and confusion caused by this struggle was over, they found that Mary, overcome with agitation and terror, was showing symptoms of fainting again, and they concluded to leave her. They informed her that she must consider herself a prisoner, and, setting a guard at the door of her apartment, they went away, leaving her to spend the night in an agony of resentment, anxiety, and fear.

Lord Darnley took the government at once entirely into his own hands. He prorogued Parliament, which was then just commencing a session, in his own name alone. He organized an administration, Mary's officers having fled. In saying that *he* did these things, we mean, of course, that the conspirators did them in his name. He was still but a boy, scarcely out of his teens, and incapable of any other action in such an emergency but a blind compliance with the wishes of the crafty men who had got him into their power by gratifying his feelings of revenge. They took possession of the government in his name, and kept Mary a close prisoner.

The murder was committed on Saturday night. The next morning, of course, was Sunday. Melville was going out of the palace about ten o'clock. As he passed along under the window where Mary was confined, she called out to him for help. He asked her what he could do for her. She told him to go to the provost of Edinburgh, the officer corresponding to the mayor of a city in this country, and ask him to call out the city guard, and come and release her from her captivity. "Go quick," said she, "or the guards will see you and stop you." Just then the guards came up and challenged Melville. He told them he was going to the city to attend church; so they let him pass on. He went to the provost, and delivered Mary's message. The provost said he dared not, and could not interfere.

So Mary remained a prisoner. Her captivity, however, was of short duration. In two days Darnley came to see her. He persuaded her that he himself had had nothing to do with the murder of Rizzio. Mary, on the other hand, persuaded him that it was better for them to be friends to each other than to live thus in a perpetual quarrel. She convinced him that Ruthven and his confederates were not, and could not be, his friends. They would only make him the instrument of obtaining the objects of their ambition. Darnley saw this. He felt that he as well as Mary were in the rebels' power. They formed a plan to escape together. They succeeded. They fled to a distant castle, and collected a large army, the people every where flocking to the assistance of the queen. They returned to Edinburgh in a short time in triumph. The conspirators fled. Mary then decided to pardon and recall the old rebels, and expend her anger henceforth on the new; and thus the Earl Murray, her brother, was brought back, and once more restored to favor.

After settling all these troubles, Mary retired to Edinburgh Castle, where it was supposed she could be best protected, and in the month of July following the murder of Rizzio, she gave birth to a son. In this son was afterward accomplished all her fondest wishes, for he inherited in the end both the English and Scottish crowns.

# 8

# Bothwell

## 1566-1567

*Earl of Bothwell.—His desperate character.—Castle of Dunbar.—The border country.—Scenes of violence and blood.—Birth of James.—Its political importance.—Darnley's conduct.—Darnley's hypocrisy.—Mary's dejection.—A divorce proposed.—Mary's love for her child.—Baptism of the infant.—James's titles.—The prince's cradle.—Bothwell and Murray. —Mary's visit to Bothwell.—Its probable motive.—Plot for Darnley's destruction.—Bothwell's intrigues.—Desperate schemes attributed to Darnley.—His illness.—Mary's visit.—Return to Edinburgh.—Situation of Darnley's residence.—Kirk of Field.—Description of Darnley's residence. —Plan of Darnley's house.—Its accommodations.—French Paris.—The gunpowder.—A wedding.—Details of the plot.—The powder placed in Mary's room.—The big cask.—Bothwell's effrontery.—Mary's leave of Darnley.—Was Mary privy to the plot?—Anecdotes of Mary.—Return to Holyrood.—French Paris falters.—The convent gardens.—Laying the train.—Suspense.—The explosion.—Flight of the criminals.—Mary's indignation.—Bothwell arrested, tried, and acquitted.—Bothwell's challenge.—His plan to marry Mary.—The abduction.—Mary's confinement at Dunbar.—Her account of it.—Bothwell entreats Mary to marry him. —She consents.—Bothwell's pardon.—The marriage.—Doubts in respect to Mary.—Influence of beauty and misfortune.*

THE Earl of Bothwell was a man of great energy of character, fearless and decided in all that he undertook, and sometimes perfectly reckless and uncontrollable. He was in Scotland at the time of Mary's return from France, but he was so turbulent and unmanageable that he was at one time sent into banishment. He was, however, afterward recalled, and again intrusted with power. He entered ardently into Mary's service in her contest with the murderers of Rizzio. He assisted her in raising an army after her flight, and in conquering Morton, Ruthven, and the rest, and driving them out of the country. Mary soon began to look upon him as, notwithstanding his roughness, her best and most efficient friend. As a reward for these services, she granted him a castle, situated in a romantic position on the eastern coast of Scotland. It was called the Castle of Dunbar. It was on a stormy promontory, overlooking the German Ocean: a very appropriate retreat and fastness for such a man of iron as he.

In those days, the border country between England and Scotland was the resort of robbers, freebooters, and outlaws from both lands. If pursued by one government, they could retreat across the line and be safe. Incursions, too, were continually made across this frontier by the people of either side, to plunder or to destroy whatever property was within reach. Thus the country became a region of violence and bloodshed which all men of peace and quietness were glad to shun. They left it to the possession of men who could find pleasure in such scenes of violence and blood. When Queen Mary had got quietly settled in her government, after the overthrow of the murderers of Rizzio, as she thus no longer needed Bothwell's immediate aid, she sent him to this border country to see if he could enforce some sort of order among its lawless population.

The birth of Mary's son was an event of the greatest importance, not only to her personally, but in respect to the political prospects of the two great kingdoms, for in this infant were combined the claims of succession to both the Scotch and English crowns. The whole world knew that if Elizabeth should die without leaving a direct heir, this child would become the monarch both of England and Scotland, and, as such, one of the greatest personages in Europe. His birth, therefore, was a great event, and it was celebrated in Scotland with universal rejoicings. The tidings of it spread, as news of great public interest, all over Europe. Even Elizabeth pretended to be pleased, and sent messages of congratulation to Mary. But every one thought that they could see in her air and manner, when she received the intelligence, obvious traces of mortification and chagrin.

Mary's heart was filled, at first, with maternal pride and joy; but her happiness was soon sadly alloyed by Darnley's continued unkindness. She traveled about during the autumn, from castle to castle, anxious and ill at ease. Sometimes Darnley followed her, and sometimes he amused himself with hunting, and with various vicious indulgences, at different towns and castles at a distance from her. He wanted her to dismiss her ministry and put him into power, and he took every possible means to importune or tease her into compliance with this plan. At one time he said he had resolved to leave Scotland, and go and reside in France, and he pretended to make his preparations, and to be about to take his leave. He seems to have thought that Mary, though he knew that she no longer loved him, would be distressed at the idea of being abandoned by one who was, after all, her husband. Mary was, in fact, distressed at this proposal, and urged him not to go. He seemed determined, and took his leave. Instead of going to France, however, he only went to Stirling Castle.

Darnley, finding that he could not accomplish his aims by such methods as these, wrote, it is said, to the Catholic governments of Europe, proposing that, if they would co-operate in putting him into power in Scotland, he would adopt efficient measures for changing the religion of the country from the Protestant to the Catholic faith. He made, too, every effort to organize a party in his favor in Scotland, and tried to defeat and counteract the influence of Mary's government by every means in his power. These things, and other trials and difficulties connected with them, weighed very heavily upon Mary's mind. She sunk gradually into a state of great dejection and despondency. She spent many hours in sighing and in tears, and often wished that she was in her grave.

So deeply, in fact, was Mary plunged into distress and trouble by the state of things existing between herself and Darnley, that some of her officers of government began to conceive of a plan of having her divorced from him. After looking at this subject in all its bearings, and consulting about it with each other, they ventured, at last, to propose it to Mary. She would not listen to any such plan. She did not think a divorce could be legally accomplished. And then, if it were to be done, it would, she feared, in some way or other, affect the position and rights of the darling son who was now to her more than all the world besides. She would rather endure to the end of her days the tyranny and torment she experienced from her brutal husband, than hazard in the least degree the future greatness and glory of the infant who was lying in his cradle before her, equally unconscious of the grandeur which awaited him in future years, and of the strength of the maternal love which was smiling upon him from amid such sorrow and tears, and extending over him such gentle, but determined and effectual protection.

The sad and sorrowful feelings which Mary endured were interrupted for a little time by the splendid pageant of the baptism of the child. Embassadors came from all the important courts of the Continent to do honor to the occasion. Elizabeth sent the Earl of Bedford as her embassador, with a present of a baptismal font of gold, which had cost a sum equal to five thousand dollars. The baptism took place at Stirling, in December, with every possible accompaniment of pomp and parade, and was followed by many days of festivities and rejoicing. The whole country were interested in the event except Darnley, who declared sullenly, while the preparations were making, that he should not remain to witness the ceremony, but should go off a day or two before the appointed time.

The ceremony was performed in the chapel. The child was baptized under the names of "Charles James, James Charles, Prince and Steward of Scotland, Duke of Rothesay, Earl of Carrick, Lord of the Isles, and Baron of Renfrew." His subsequent designation in history was James Sixth of Scotland and First of England. A great many appointments of attendants and officers, to be attached to the service of the young prince, were made immediately, most of them, of course, mere matters of parade. Among the rest, five ladies of distinction were constituted "rockers of his cradle." The form of the young prince's cradle has come down to us in an ancient drawing.

Prince James's Cradle

In due time after the coronation, the various embassadors and delegates returned to their respective courts, carrying back glowing accounts of the ceremonies and festivities attendant upon the christening, and of the grace, and beauty, and loveliness of the queen.

In the mean time, Bothwell and Murray were competitors for the confidence and regard of the queen, and it began to seem probable that Bothwell would win the day. Mary, in one of her excursions, was traveling in the southern part of the country, when she heard that he had been wounded in an encounter with a party of desperadoes near the border. Moved partly, perhaps, by compassion, and partly by gratitude for his services, Mary made an expedition across the country to pay him a visit. Some say that she was animated by a more powerful motive than either of these. In fact this, as well as almost all the other acts of Mary's life, are presented in very different lights by her friends and her enemies. The former say that this visit to her lieutenant in his confinement from a wound received in her service was perfectly proper, both in the design itself, and in all the circumstances of its execution. The latter represent it as an instance of highly indecorous eagerness on the part of a married lady to express to another man a sympathy and kind regard which she had ceased to feel for her husband.

Bothwell himself was married as well as Mary. He had been married but a few months to a beautiful lady a few years younger than the queen. The question, however, whether Mary did right or wrong in paying this visit to him, is not, after all, a very important one. There is no doubt that she and Bothwell loved each other before they ought to have done so, and it is of comparatively little consequence when the attachment began. The end of it is certain. Bothwell resolved to kill Darnley, to get divorced from his own wife, and to marry the queen. The world has never yet settled the question whether she was herself his accomplice or not in the measures he adopted for effecting these plans, or whether she only submitted to the result when Bothwell, by his own unaided efforts, reached it. Each reader must judge of this question for himself from the facts about to be narrated.

Bothwell first communicated with the nobles about the court, to get their consent and approbation to the destruction of the king. They all appeared to be very willing to have the thing done, but were a little cautious about involving themselves in the responsibility of doing it. Darnley was thoroughly hated, despised, and shunned by them all. Still they were afraid of the consequences of taking his life. One of them, Morton, asked Bothwell what the queen would think of the plan. Bothwell said that the queen approved of it. Morton replied, that if Bothwell would show him an expression of the queen's approval of the plot, in her own hand-writing, he would join it, otherwise not. Bothwell failed to furnish this evidence, saying that the queen was really privy to, and in favor of the plan, but that it was not to be expected that she would commit herself to it in writing. Was this all true, or was the pretense only a desperate measure of Bothwell's to induce Morton to join him?

Most of the leading men about the court, however, either joined the plot, or so far gave it their countenance and encouragement as to induce Bothwell to proceed. There were many and strange rumors about Darnley. One was, that he was actually going to leave the country, and that a ship was ready for him in the Clyde. Another was, that he had a plan for seizing the young prince, dethroning Mary, and reigning himself in her stead, in the prince's name. Other strange and desperate schemes were attributed to him. In the midst of them, news came to Mary at Holyrood that he was taken suddenly and dangerously sick at Glasgow, where he was then residing, and she immediately went to see him. Was her motive a desire to make one more attempt to win his confidence and love, and to divert him from the desperate measures which she feared he was contemplating, or was she acting as an accomplice with Bothwell, to draw him into the snare in which he was afterward taken and destroyed?

The result of Mary's visit to her husband, after some time spent with him in Glasgow, was a proposal that he should return with her to Edinburgh, where she could watch over him during his convalescence with greater care. This plan was adopted. He was conveyed on a sort of litter, by very slow and easy stages, toward Edinburgh. He was on such terms with the nobles and lords in attendance upon Mary that he was not willing to go to Holyrood House. Besides, his disorder was contagious: it is supposed to have been the small-pox; and though he was nearly recovered, there was still some possibility that the royal babe might take the infection if the patient came within the same walls with him. So Mary sent forward to Edinburgh to have a house provided for him.

The situation of this house is seen near the city wall on the left, in the accompanying view of Edinburgh. Holyrood House is the large square edifice in the fore-ground, and the castle crowns the hill in the distance. There is now, as there was in the days of Mary, a famous street extending from Holyrood House to the castle, called the Cannon Gate at the lower end, and the High Street above. This street, with the castle at one extremity and Holyrood House at the other, were the scenes of many of the most remarkable events described in this narrative.

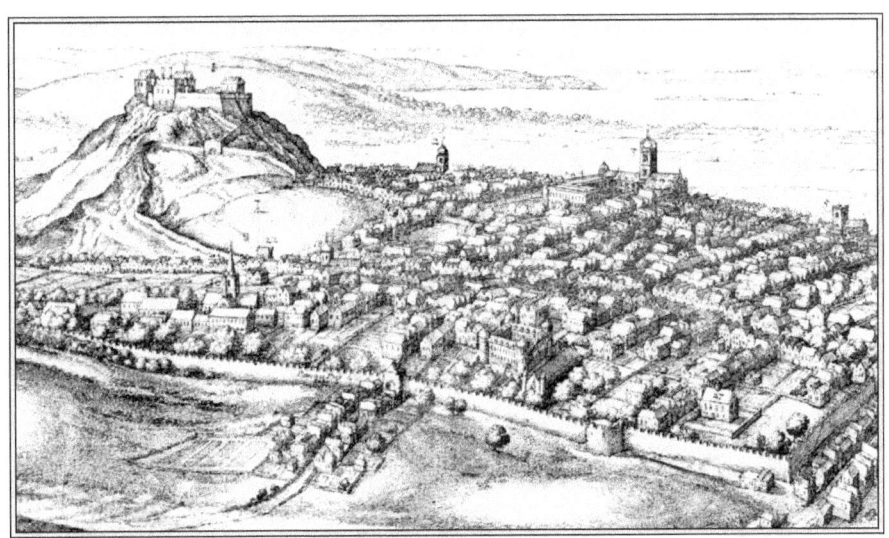

View of Edinburgh

The residence selected was a house of four rooms, close upon the city wall. The place was called the Kirk of Field, from a *kirk*, or church, which formerly stood near there, in the fields.

This house had two rooms upon the lower floor, with a passage-way between them. One of these rooms was a kitchen; the other was appropriated to Mary's use, whenever she was able to be at the place in attendance upon her husband. Over the kitchen was a room used as a wardrobe and for servants; and over Mary's room was the apartment for Darnley. There was an opening through the city wall in the rear of this dwelling, by which there was access to the kitchen. These premises were fitted up for Darnley in the most thorough manner. A bath was arranged for him in his apartment, and every thing was done which could conduce to his comfort, according to the ideas which then prevailed. Darnley was brought to Edinburgh, conveyed to this house, and quietly established there.

The following is a plan of the house in which Darnley was lodged:

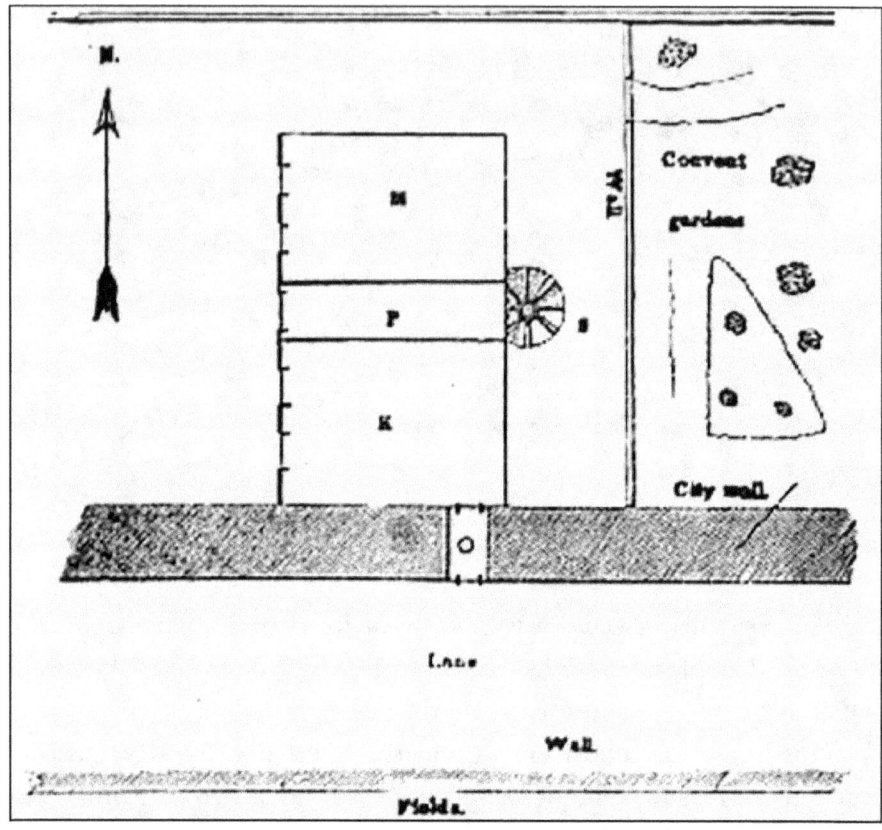

Plan of The House at the Kirk o' Field

*M. Mary's room, below Darnley's. K. Kitchen; servants' room above. O. Passage through the city wall into the kitchen. S. Staircase leading to the second story. P. Passage-way.*

The accommodations in this house do not seem to have been very sumptuous, after all, for a royal guest; but royal dwellings in Scotland, in those days, were not what they are now in Westminster and at St. Cloud.

The day for the execution of the plan, which was to blow up the house where the sick Darnley was lying with gunpowder, approached. Bothwell selected a number of desperate characters to aid him in the actual work to be done. One of these was a Frenchman, who had been for a long time in his service, and who went commonly by the name of French Paris. Bothwell contrived to get French Paris taken into Mary's service a few days before the murder of Darnley, and, through him, he got possession of some of the keys of the house which Darnley was occupying, and thus had duplicates of them made, so that he had access to every part of the house. The gunpowder was brought from Bothwell's castle at Dunbar, and all was ready.

Mary spent much of her time at Darnley's house, and often slept in the room beneath his, which had been allotted to her as her apartment. One Sunday there was to be a wedding at Holyrood. The bride and bridegroom were favorite servants of Mary's, and she was intending to be present at the celebration of the nuptials. She was to leave Darnley's early in the evening for this purpose. Her enemies say that this was all a concerted arrangement between her and Bothwell to give him the opportunity to execute his plan. Her friends, on the other hand, insist that she knew nothing about it, and that Bothwell had to watch and wait for such an opportunity of blowing up the house without injuring Mary. Be this as it may, the Sunday of this wedding was fixed upon for the consummation of the deed.

The gunpowder had been secreted in Bothwell's rooms at the palace. On Sunday evening, as soon as it was dark, Bothwell set the men at work to transport the gunpowder. They brought it out in bags from the palace, and then employed a horse to transport it to the wall of some gardens which were in the rear of Darnley's house. They had to go twice with the horse in order to convey all the gunpowder that they had provided. While this was going on, Bothwell, who kept out of sight, was walking to and fro in an adjoining street, to receive intelligence, from time to time, of the progress of the affair, and to issue orders. The gunpowder was conveyed across the gardens to the rear of the house, taken in at a back door, and deposited in the room marked *M* in the plan, which was the room belonging to Mary. Mary was all this time directly over head, in Darnley's chamber.

The plan of the conspirators was to put the bags of gunpowder into a cask which they had provided for the occasion, to keep the mass together, and increase the force of the explosion. The cask had been provided, and placed in the gardens behind the house; but, on attempting to take it into the house, they found it too big to pass through the back door. This caused considerable delay; and Bothwell, growing impatient, came, with his characteristic impetuosity, to ascertain the cause. By his presence and his energy, he soon remedied the difficulty in some way or other, and completed the arrangements. The gunpowder was all deposited; the men were dismissed, except two who were left to watch, and who were locked up with the gunpowder in Mary's room; and then, all things being ready for the explosion as soon as Mary should be gone, Bothwell walked up to Darnley's room above, and joined the party who were supping there. The cool effrontery of this proceeding has scarcely a parallel in the annals of crime.

At eleven o'clock Mary rose to go, saying she must return to the palace to take part, as she had promised to do, in the celebration of her servants' wedding. Mary took leave of her husband in a very affectionate manner, and went away in company with Bothwell and the other nobles. Her enemies maintain that she was privy to all the arrangements which had been made, and that she did not go into her own apartment below, knowing very well what was there. But even if we imagine that Mary was aware of the general plan of destroying her husband, and was secretly pleased with it, as almost any royal personage that ever lived, under such circumstances, would be, we need not admit that she was acquainted with the details of the mode by which the plan was to be put in execution. The most that we can suppose such a man as Bothwell would have communicated to her, would be some dark and obscure intimations of his design, made in order to satisfy himself that she would not really oppose it. To ask her, woman as she was, to take any part in such a deed, or to communicate to her beforehand any of the details of the arrangement, would have been an act of littleness and meanness which such magnanimous monsters as Bothwell are seldom guilty of.

Besides, Mary remarked that evening, in Darnley's room, in the course of conversation, that it was just about a year since Rizzio's death. On entering her palace, too, at Holyrood, that night, she met one of Bothwell's servants who had been carrying the bags, and, perceiving the smell of gunpowder, she asked him what it meant. Now Mary was not the brazen-faced sort of woman to speak of such things at such a time if she was really in the councils of the conspirators. The only question seems to be, therefore, not whether she was a party to the actual deed of murder, but only whether she was aware of, and consenting to, the general design.

In the mean time, Mary and Bothwell went together into the hall where the servants were rejoicing and making merry at the wedding. French Paris was there, but his heart began to fail him in respect to the deed in which he had been engaged. He stood apart, with a countenance expressive of anxiety and distress. Bothwell went to him, and told him that if he carried such a melancholy face as that any longer in the presence of the queen, he would make him suffer for it. The poor conscience-stricken man begged Bothwell to release him from any further part in the transaction. He was sick, really sick, he said, and he wanted to go home to his bed. Bothwell made no reply but to order him to follow *him*. Bothwell went to his own rooms, changed the silken court dress in which he had appeared in company for one suitable to the night and to the deed, directed his men to follow him, and passed from the palace toward the gates of the city. The gates were shut, for it was midnight. The sentinels challenged them. The party said they were friends to my Lord Bothwell, and were allowed to pass on.

They advanced to the convent gardens. Here they left a part of their number, while Bothwell and French Paris passed over the wall, and crept softly into the house. They unlocked the room where they had left the two watchmen with the gunpowder, and found all safe. Men locked up under such circumstances, and on the eve of the perpetration of such a deed, were not likely to sleep at their posts. All things being now ready, they made a slow match of lint, long enough to burn for some little time, and inserting one end of it into the gunpowder, they lighted the other end, and crept stealthily out of the apartment. They passed over the wall into the convent gardens, where they rejoined their companions and awaited the result.

Men choose midnight often for the perpetration of crime, from the facilities afforded by its silence and solitude. This advantage is, however, sometimes well-nigh balanced by the stimulus which its mysterious solemnity brings to the stings of remorse and terror. Bothwell himself felt anxious and agitated. They waited and waited, but it seemed as if their dreadful suspense would never end. Bothwell became desperate. He wanted to get over the wall again and look in at the window, to see if the slow match had not gone out. The rest restrained him. At length the explosion came like a clap of thunder. The flash brightened for an instant over the whole sky, and the report roused the sleeping inhabitants of Edinburgh from their slumbers, throwing the whole city into sudden consternation.

The perpetrators of the deed, finding that their work was done, fled immediately. They tried various plans to avoid the sentinels at the gates of the city, as well as the persons who were beginning to come toward the scene of the explosion. When they reached the palace of Holyrood, they were challenged by the sentinel on duty there. They said that they were friends of Earl Bothwell, bringing dispatches to him from the country. The sentinel asked them if they knew what was the cause of that loud explosion. They said they did not, and passed on.

Bothwell went to his room, called for a drink, undressed himself, and went to bed. Half an hour afterward, messengers came to awaken him, and inform him that the king's house had been blown up with gunpowder, and the king himself killed by the explosion. He rose with an appearance of great astonishment and indignation, and, after conferring with some of the other nobles, concluded to go and communicate the event to the queen. The queen was overwhelmed with astonishment and indignation too.

The destruction of Darnley in such a manner as this, of course produced a vast sensation all over Scotland. Every body was on the alert to discover the authors of the crime. Rewards were offered; proclamations were made. Rumors began to circulate that Bothwell was the criminal. He was accused by anonymous placards put up at night in Edinburgh. Lennox, Darnley's father, demanded his trial; and a trial was ordered. The circumstances of the trial were such, however, and Bothwell's power and desperate recklessness were so great, that Lennox, when the time came, did not appear. He said he had not *force enough* at his command to come safely into court. There being no testimony offered, Bothwell was acquitted; and he immediately afterward issued his proclamation, offering to fight any man who should intimate, in any way, that he was concerned in the murder of the king. Thus Bothwell established his innocence; at least, no man dared to gainsay it.

Darnley was murdered in February. Bothwell was tried and acquitted in April. Immediately afterward, he took measures for privately making known to the leading nobles that it was his design to marry the queen, and for securing their concurrence in the plan. They concurred; or at least, perhaps for fear of displeasing such a desperado, said what he understood to mean that they concurred. The queen heard the reports of such a design, and said, as ladies often do in similar cases, that she did not know what people meant by such reports; there was no foundation for them whatever.

Toward the end of April, Mary was about returning from the castle of Stirling to Edinburgh with a small escort of troops and attendants. Melville was in her train. Bothwell set out at the head of a force of more than five hundred men to intercept her. Mary lodged one night, on her way, at Linlithgow, the palace where she was born, and the next morning was quietly pursuing her journey, when Bothwell came up at the head of his troops. Resistance was vain. Bothwell advanced to Mary's horse, and, taking the bridle, led her away. A few of her principal followers were taken prisoners too, and the rest were dismissed. Bothwell took his captive across the country by a rapid flight to his castle of Dunbar. The attendants who were taken with her were released, and she remained in the Castle of Dunbar for ten days, entirely in Bothwell's power.

Dunbar Castle—The Residence of Earl Bothwell

According to the account which Mary herself gives of what took place during this captivity, she at first reproached Bothwell bitterly for the ungrateful and cruel return he was making for all her kindness to him, by such a deed of violence and wrong, and begged and entreated him to let her go. Bothwell replied that he knew that it was wrong for him to treat his sovereign so rudely, but that he was impelled to it by the circumstances of the case, and by love which he felt for her, which was too strong for him to control. He then entreated her to become his wife; he complained of the bitter hostility which he had always been subject to from his enemies, and that he could have no safeguard from this hostility in time to come but in her favor; and he could not depend upon any assurance of her favor less than her making him her husband. He protested that, if she would do so, he would never ask to share her power, but would be content to be her faithful and devoted servant, as he had always been. It was love, not ambition, he said, that animated him, and he could not and would not be refused. Mary says that she was distressed and agitated beyond measure by the appeals and threats with which Bothwell accompanied his urgent entreaties. She tried every way to plan some mode of escape. Nobody came to her rescue. She was entirely alone, and in Bothwell's power. Bothwell assured her that the leading nobles of her court were in favor of the marriage, and showed her a written agreement signed by them to this effect. At length, wearied and exhausted, she was finally overcome by his urgency, and yielding partly to his persuasions, and partly, as she says, to force, gave herself up to his power.

Mary remained at Dunbar about ten days, during which time Bothwell sued out and obtained a divorce from his wife. His wife, feeling, perhaps, resentment more than grief, sued, at the same time, for a divorce from him. Bothwell then sallied forth from his fastness at Dunbar, and, taking Mary with him, went to Edinburgh, and took up his abode in the castle there, as that fortress was then under his power. Mary soon after appeared in public and stated that she was now entirely free, and that, although Bothwell had done wrong in carrying her away by violence, still he had treated her since in so respectful a manner, that she had pardoned him, and had received him into favor again. A short time after this they were married. The ceremony was performed in a very private and unostentatious manner, and took place in May, about three months after the murder of Darnley.

By some persons Mary's account of the transactions at Dunbar is believed. Others think that the whole affair was all a preconcerted plan, and that the appearance of resistance on her part was only for show, to justify, in some degree, in the eyes of the world, so imprudent and inexcusable a marriage. A great many volumes have been written on the question without making any progress toward a settlement of it. It is one of those cases where, the evidence being complicated, conflicting, and incomplete, the mind is swayed by the feelings, and the readers of the story decide more or less favorably for the unhappy queen, according to the warmth of the interest awakened in their hearts by beauty and misfortune.

# 9

# The Fall of Bothwell

### 1567

*Mary's infatuation.—Excuses for her.—Mary's deep depression.—Interposition of the King of France.—Bothwell at Edinburgh Castle.—He is hated by the people.—The opposing parties.—How far Mary was responsible.—Melrose.—Ruins of the abbey.—Mary's proclamation.—The prince's lords.—Bothwell alarmed.—Borthwick Castle.—Bothwell's retreat.—He is besieged.—Makes his escape.—Bothwell at Dunbar.—Proclamation.—Approaching contest.—Mary's appeal.—Approach of the prince's lords.—Carberry Hill.—Efforts of Le Croc to effect an accommodation.—Bothwell's challenge.—Morton.—Mary sends for Grange.—Proposition of Grange.—Dismissal of Bothwell.—Question of Mary's guilt.—The supposition against her.—The supposition in her favor.—Uncertainty.—The box of love letters.—Their genuineness suspected.—Disposal of Mary.—Return to Edinburgh.—The banner.—Rudeness of the populace.—Bothwell's retreat.—He is pursued.—Bothwell's narrow escape.—He turns pirate.—Bothwell in prison.—His miserable end.*

THE course which Mary pursued after her liberation from Dunbar in yielding to Bothwell's wishes, pardoning his violence, receiving him again into favor, and becoming his wife, is one of the most extraordinary instances of the infatuation produced by love that has ever occurred. If the story had been fiction instead of truth, it would have been pronounced extravagant and impossible. As it was, the whole country was astonished and confounded at such a rapid succession of desperate and unaccountable crimes. Mary herself seems to have been hurried through these terrible scenes in a sort of delirium of excitement, produced by the strange circumstances of the case, and the wild and uncontrollable agitations to which they gave rise.

Such was, however, at the time, and such continues to be still, the feeling of interest in Mary's character and misfortunes, that but few open and direct censures of her conduct were then, or have been since, expressed. People execrated Bothwell, but they were silent in respect to Mary. It was soon plain, however, that she had greatly sunk in their regard, and that the more they reflected upon the circumstances of the case, the deeper she was sinking. When the excitement, too, began to pass away from her own mind, it left behind it a gnawing inquietude and sense of guilt, which grew gradually more and more intense, until, at length, she sunk under the stings of remorse and despair.

Her sufferings were increased by the evidences which were continually coming to her mind of the strong degree of disapprobation with which her conduct began soon every where to be regarded. Wherever Scotchmen traveled, they found themselves reproached with the deeds of violence and crime of which their country had been the scene. Mary's relatives and friends in France wrote to her, expressing their surprise and grief at such proceedings. The King of France had sent, a short time before, a special embassador for the purpose of doing something, if possible, to discover and punish the murderers of Darnley. His name was Le Croc. He was an aged and venerable man, of great prudence and discretion, well qualified to discover and pursue the way of escape from the difficulties in which Mary had involved herself, if any such way could be found. He arrived before the day of Mary's marriage, but he refused to take any part, or even to be present, at the ceremony.

In the mean time, Bothwell continued in Edinburgh Castle for a while, under the protection of a strong guard. People considered this guard as intended to prevent Mary's escape, and many thought that she was detained, after all, against her will, and that her admissions that she was free were only made at the instigation of Bothwell, and from fear of his terrible power. The other nobles and the people of Scotland began to grow more and more uneasy. The fear of Bothwell began to be changed into hatred, and the more powerful nobles commenced forming plans for combining together, and rescuing, as they said, Mary out of his power.

Bothwell made no attempts to conciliate them. He assumed an air and tone of defiance. He increased his forces. He conceived the plan of going to Stirling Castle to seize the young prince, who was residing there under the charge of persons to whom his education had been intrusted. He said to his followers that James should never do any thing to avenge his father's death, if he could once get him into his hands. The other nobles formed a league to counteract these designs. They began to assemble their forces, and every thing threatened an outbreak of civil war.

The marriage took place about the middle of May, and within a fortnight from that time the lines began to be pretty definitely drawn between the two great parties, the queen and Bothwell on one side, and the insurgent nobles on the other, each party claiming to be friends of the queen. Whatever was done on Bothwell's side was, of course, in the queen's name, though it is very doubtful how far she was responsible for what was done, or how far, on the other hand, she merely aided, under the influence of a species of compulsion, in carrying into execution Bothwell's measures. We must say, in narrating the history, that the queen did this and that, and must leave the reader to judge whether it was herself, or Bothwell acting through her, who was the real agent in the transactions described.

Stirling Castle, where the young prince was residing, is northwest of Edinburgh. The confederate lords were assembling in that vicinity. The border country between England and Scotland is of course south. In the midst of this border country is the ancient town of Melrose, where there was, in former days, a very rich and magnificent abbey, the ruins of which, to this day, form one of the most attractive objects of interest in the whole island of Great Britain. The region is now the abode of peace, and quietness, and plenty, though in Mary's day it was the scene of continual turmoil and war. It is now the favorite retreat of poets and philosophers, who seek their residences there on account of its stillness and peace. Sir Walter Scott's Abbotsford is a few miles from Melrose.

About a fortnight after Mary's marriage, she issued a proclamation ordering the military chiefs in her kingdom to assemble at Melrose, with their followers, to accompany her on an expedition through the border country, to suppress some disorders there. The nobles considered this as only a scheme of Bothwell's to draw them away from the neighborhood of Stirling, so that he might go and get possession of the young prince. Rumors of this spread around the country, and the forces, instead of proceeding to Melrose, began to assemble in the neighborhood of Stirling, for the protection of the prince. The lords under whose banners they gathered assumed the name of *the prince's* lords, and they called upon the people to take up arms in defense of young James's person and rights. The prince's lords soon began to concentrate their forces about Edinburgh, and Bothwell was alarmed for his safety. He had reason to fear that the governor of Edinburgh Castle was on their side, and that he might suddenly sally forth with a body of his forces down the High Street to Holyrood, and take him prisoner. He accordingly began to think it necessary to retreat.

Now Bothwell had, among his other possessions, a certain castle called Borthwick Castle, a few miles south of Edinburgh. It was situated on a little swell of land in a beautiful valley. It was surrounded with groves of trees, and from the windows and walls of the castle there was an extended view over the beautiful and fertile fields of the valley. This castle was extensive and strong. It consisted of one great square tower, surrounded and protected by walls and bastions, and was approached by a draw-bridge. In the sudden emergency in which Bothwell found himself placed, this fortress seemed to be the most convenient and the surest retreat. On the 6th of June, he accordingly left Edinburgh with as large a force as he had at command, and rode rapidly across the country with the queen, and established himself at Borthwick.

The prince's lords, taking fresh courage from the evidence of Bothwell's weakness and fear, immediately marched from Stirling, passed by Edinburgh, and almost immediately after Bothwell and the queen had got safely, as they imagined, established in the place of their retreat, they found their castle surrounded and hemmed in on all sides by hostile forces, which filled the whole valley. The castle was strong, but not strong enough to withstand a siege from such an army. Bothwell accordingly determined to retreat to his castle of Dunbar, which, being on a rocky promontory, jutting into the sea, and more remote from the heart of the country, was less accessible, and more safe than Borthwick. He contrived, though with great difficulty, to make his escape with the queen, through the ranks of his enemies. It is said that the queen was disguised in male attire. At any rate, they made their escape, they reached Dunbar, and Mary, or Bothwell in her name, immediately issued a proclamation, calling upon all her faithful subjects to assemble in arms, to deliver her from her dangers. At the same time, the prince's lords issued *their* proclamation, calling upon all faithful subjects to assemble with them, to aid them in delivering the queen from the tyrant who held her captive.

The faithful subjects were at a loss which proclamation to obey. By far the greater number joined the insurgents. Some thousands, however, went to Dunbar. With this force the queen and Bothwell sallied forth, about the middle of June, to meet the prince's lords, or the insurgents, as they called them, to settle the question at issue by the kind of ballot with which such questions were generally settled in those days.

Mary had a proclamation read at the head of her army, now that she supposed she was on the eve of battle, in which she explained the causes of the quarrel. The proclamation stated that the marriage was Mary's free act, and that, although it was in some respects an extraordinary one, still the circumstances were such that she could not do otherwise than she had done. For ten days she had been in Bothwell's power in his castle at Dunbar, and not an arm had been raised for her deliverance. Her subjects ought to have interposed then, if they were intending really to rescue her from Bothwell's power. They had done nothing then, but now, when she had been compelled, by the cruel circumstances of her condition, to marry Bothwell—when the act was done, and could no longer be recalled, they had taken up arms against her, and compelled her to take the field in her own defense.

The army of the prince's lords, with Mary's most determined enemies at their head, advanced to meet the queen's forces. The queen finally took her post on an elevated piece of ground called Carberry Hill. Carberry is an old Scotch name for gooseberry. Carberry Hill is a few miles to the eastward of Edinburgh, near Dalkeith. Here the two armies were drawn up, opposite to each other, in hostile array.

Le Croc, the aged and venerable French embassador, made a great effort to effect an accommodation and prevent a battle. He first went to the queen and obtained authority from her to offer terms of peace, and then went to the camp of the prince's lords and proposed that they should lay down their arms and submit to the queen's authority, and that she would forgive and forget what they had done. They replied that they had done no wrong, and asked for no pardon; that they were not in arms against the queen's authority, but in favor of it. They sought only to deliver her from the durance in which she was held, and to bring to punishment the murderers of her husband, whoever they might be. Le Croc went back and forth several times, vainly endeavoring to effect an accommodation, and finally, giving up in despair, he returned to Edinburgh, leaving the contending parties to settle the contest in their own way.

Bothwell now sent a herald to the camp of his enemies, challenging any one of them to meet him, and settle the question of his guilt or innocence by single combat. This proposition was not quite so absurd in those days as it would be now, for it was not an uncommon thing, in the Middle Ages, to try in this way questions of crime. Many negotiations ensued on Bothwell's proposal. One or two persons expressed themselves ready to accept the challenge. Bothwell objected to them on account of their rank being inferior to his, but said he would fight Morton, if Morton would accept his challenge. Morton had been his accomplice in the murder of Darnley, but had afterward joined the party of Bothwell's foes. It would have been a singular spectacle to see one of these confederates in the commission of a crime contending desperately in single combat to settle the question of the guilt or innocence of the other.

The combat, however, did not take place. After many negotiations on the subject, the plan was abandoned, each party charging the other with declining the contest. The queen and Bothwell, in the mean time, found such evidences of strength on the part of their enemies, and felt probably, in their own hearts, so much of that faintness and misgiving under which human energy almost always sinks when the tide begins to turn against it, after the commission of wrong, that they began to feel disheartened and discouraged. The queen sent to the opposite camp with a request that a certain personage, the Laird of Grange, in whom all parties had great confidence, should come to her, that she might make one more effort at reconciliation. Grange, after consulting with the prince's lords, made a proposition to Mary, which she finally concluded to accept. It was as follows:

They proposed that Mary should come over to their camp, not saying very distinctly whether she was to come as their captive or as their queen. The event showed that it was in the former capacity that they intended to receive her, though they were probably willing that she should understand that it was in the latter. At all events, the proposition itself did not make it very clear what her position would be; and the poor queen, distracted by the difficulties which surrounded her, and overwhelmed with agitation and fear, could not press very strongly for precise stipulations. In respect to Bothwell, they compromised the question by agreeing that, as he was under suspicion in respect to the murder of Darnley, he should not accompany the queen, but should be dismissed upon the field; that is, allowed to depart, without molestation, wherever he should choose to go. This plan was finally adopted. The queen bade Bothwell farewell, and he went away reluctantly and in great apparent displeasure. He had, in fact, with his characteristic ferocity, attempted to shoot Grange pending the negotiation. He mounted his horse, and, with a few attendants, rode off and sought a retreat once more upon his rock at Dunbar.

From all the evidence which has come down to us, it seems impossible to ascertain whether Mary desired to be released from Bothwell's power, and was glad when the release came, or whether she still loved him, and was planning a reunion, so soon as a reunion should be possible. One party at that time maintained, and a large class of writers and readers since have concurred in the opinion, that Mary was in love with Bothwell before Darnley's death; that she connived with him in the plan for Darnley's murder; that she was a consenting party to the abduction, and the spending of the ten days at Dunbar Castle, in his power; that the marriage was the end at which she herself, as well as Bothwell, had been all the time aiming; and then, when at last she surrendered herself to the prince's lords at Carberry Hill, it was only yielding unwillingly to the necessity of a temporary separation from her lawless husband, with a view of reinstating him in favor and power at the earliest opportunity.

Another party, both among her people at the time and among the writers and readers who have since paid attention to her story, think that she never loved Bothwell, and that, though she valued his services as a bold and energetic soldier, she had no collusion with him whatever in respect to Darnley's murder. They think that, though she must have felt in some sense relieved of a burden by Darnley's death, she did not in any degree aid in or justify the crime, and that she had no reason for supposing that Bothwell had any share in the commission of it. They think, also, that her consenting to marry Bothwell is to be accounted for by her natural desire to seek shelter, under some wing or other, from the terrible storms which were raging around her; and being deserted, as she thought, by every body else, and moved by his passionate love and devotion, she imprudently gave herself to him; that she lamented the act as soon as it was done, but that it was then too late to retrieve the step; and that, harassed and in despair, she knew not what to do, but that she hailed the rising of her nobles as affording the only promise of deliverance, and came forth from Dunbar to meet them with the secret purpose of delivering herself into their hands.

The question which of these two suppositions is the correct one has been discussed a great deal, without the possibility of arriving at any satisfactory conclusion. A parcel of letters were produced by Mary's enemies, some time after this, which they said were Mary's letters to Bothwell before her husband Darnley's death. They say they took the letters from a man named Dalgleish, one of Bothwell's servants, who was carrying them from Holyrood to Dunbar Castle, just after Mary and Bothwell fled to Borthwick. They were contained in a small gilded box or coffer, with the letter F upon it, under a crown; which mark naturally suggests to our minds Mary's first husband, Francis, the king of France. Dalgleish said that Bothwell sent him for this box, charging him to convey it with all care to Dunbar Castle. The letters purport to be from Mary to Bothwell, and to have been written before Darnley's death. They evince a strong affection for the person to whom they are addressed, and seem conclusively to prove the unlawful attachment between the parties, provided that their genuineness is acknowledged. But this genuineness is denied. Mary's friends maintain that they are forgeries, prepared by her enemies to justify their own wrong. Many volumes have been written on the question of the genuineness of these love letters, as they are called, and there is perhaps now no probability that the question will ever be settled.

Whatever doubt there may be about these things, there is none about the events which followed. After Mary had surrendered herself to her nobles they took her to the camp, she herself riding on horseback, and Grange walking by her side. As she advanced to meet the nobles who had combined against her, she said to them that she had concluded to come over to them, not from fear, or from doubt what the issue would have been if she had fought the battle, but only because she wanted to spare the effusion of Christian blood, especially the blood of her own subjects. She had therefore decided to submit herself to their counsels, trusting that they would treat her as their rightful queen. The nobles made little reply to this address, but prepared to return to Edinburgh with their prize.

The people of Edinburgh, who had heard what turn the affair had taken, flocked out upon the roads to see the queen return. They lined the waysides to gaze upon the great cavalcade as it passed. The nobles who conducted Mary thus back toward her capital had a banner prepared, or allowed one to be prepared, on which was a painting representing the dead body of Darnley, and the young prince James kneeling near him, and calling on God to avenge his cause. Mary came on, in the procession, after this symbol. They might perhaps say that it was not intended to wound her feelings, and was not of a nature to do it, unless she considered herself as taking sides with the murderers of her husband. She, however, knew very well that she was so regarded by great numbers of the populace assembled, and that the effect of such an effigy carried before her was to hold her up to public obloquy. The populace did, in fact, taunt and reproach her as she proceeded, and she rode into Edinburgh, evincing all the way extreme mental suffering by her agitation and her tears.

She expected that they were at least to take her to Holyrood; but no, they turned at the gate to enter the city. Mary protested earnestly against this, and called, half frantic, on all who heard her to come to her rescue. But no one interfered. They took her to the provost's house, and lodged her there for the night, and the crowd which had assembled to observe these proceedings gradually dispersed. There seemed, however, in a day or two, to be some symptoms of a reaction in favor of the fallen queen; and, to guard against the possibility of a rescue, the lords took

Mary to Holyrood again, and began immediately to make arrangements for some more safe place of confinement still.

In the mean time, Bothwell went from Carberry Hill to his castle at Dunbar, revolving moodily in his mind his altered fortunes. After some time he found himself not safe in this place of refuge, and so he retreated to the north, to some estates he had there, in the remote Highlands. A detachment of forces was sent in pursuit of him. Now there are, north of Scotland, some groups of dismal islands, the summits of submerged mountains and rocks, rising in dark and sublime, but gloomy grandeur, from the midst of cold and tempestuous seas. Bothwell, finding himself pursued, undertook to escape by ship to these islands. His pursuers, headed by Grange, who had negotiated at Carberry for the surrender of the queen, embarked in other vessels, and pressed on after him. At one time they almost overtook him, and would have captured him and all his company were it not that they got entangled among some shoals. Grange's sailors said they must not proceed. Grange, eager to seize his prey, insisted on their making sail and pressing forward. The consequence was, they ran the vessels aground, and Bothwell escaped in a small boat. As it was, however, they seized some of his accomplices, and brought them back to Edinburgh. These men were afterward tried, and some of them were executed; and it was at their trial, and through the confessions they made, that the facts were brought to light which have been related in this narrative.

Bothwell, now a fugitive and an exile, but still retaining his desperate and lawless character, became a pirate, and attempted to live by robbing the commerce of the German Ocean. Rumor is the only historian, in ordinary cases, to record the events in the life of a pirate; and she, in this case, sent word, from time to time, to Scotland, of the robberies and murders that the desperado committed; of an expedition fitted out against him by the King of Denmark, of his being taken and carried into a Danish port; of his being held in imprisonment for a long period there, in a gloomy dungeon; of his restless spirit chafing itself in useless struggles against his fate, and sinking gradually, at last under the burdens of remorse for past crimes, and despair of any earthly deliverance; of his insanity, and, finally, of his miserable end.

# 10

## Loch Leven Castle

### 1567-1568

*Grange of Kircaldy.—Mary's letter.—Removal of Mary.—A ride at night.—Loch Leven Castle.—The square tower.—Plan of Loch Leven Castle.—Lady Douglas.—Lady Douglas Mary's enemy.—Parties for and against Mary.—The Hamilton lords.—Plans of Mary's enemies. —Mary's tower.—Ruins.—The scale turns against Mary.—Proposals made to Mary.—The commissioners.—Melville unsuccessful.—Lindsay called in.—Lindsay's brutality.—Abdication.—Coronation of James.— Ceremonies.—Return of Murray.—Murray's interview with Mary.— Affecting scene.—Murray assumes the government.—His warnings.— The young Douglases.—Their interest in Mary.—Plan for Mary's escape. —The laundress.—The disguise.—Escape.—Discovery.—Mary's return. —Banishment of George Douglas.—Secret communications.—New plan of escape.—The postern gate.—Liberation of Mary.—Jane Kennedy.— The escape.—Mary's joy.—Popular feeling.—Mary's proclamation.— Ruins of Loch Leven Castle.—The octagonal tower.—Visitors.*

GRANGE, or, as he is sometimes called, Kircaldy, his title in full being Grange of Kircaldy, was a man of integrity and honor, and he, having been the negotiator through whose intervention Mary gave herself up, felt himself bound to see that the stipulations on the part of the nobles should be honorably fulfilled. He did all in his power to protect Mary from insult on the journey, and he struck with his sword and drove away some of the populace who were addressing her with taunts and reproaches. When he found that the nobles were confining her, and treating her so much more like a captive than like a queen, he remonstrated with them. They silenced him by showing him a letter, which they said they had intercepted on its way from Mary to Bothwell. It was written, they said, on the night of Mary's arrival at Edinburgh. It assured Bothwell that she retained an unaltered affection for him; that her consenting to be separated from him at Carberry Hill was a matter of mere necessity, and that she should rejoin him as soon as it was in her power to do so. This letter showed, they said, that, after all, Mary was not, as they had supposed, Bothwell's captive and victim, but that she was his accomplice and friend; and that, now that they had discovered their mistake, they must treat Mary, as well as Bothwell, as an enemy, and take effectual means to protect themselves from the one as well as from the other. Mary's friends maintain that this letter was a forgery.

They accordingly took Mary, as has been already stated, from the provost's house in Edinburgh down to Holyrood House, which was just without the city. This, however, was only a temporary change. That night they came into the palace, and directed Mary to rise and put on a traveling dress which they brought her. They did not tell her where she was to go, but simply ordered her to follow them. It was midnight. They took her forth from the palace, mounted her upon a horse, and, with Ruthven and Lindsay, two of the murderers of Rizzio, for an escort, they rode away. They traveled all night, crossed the River Forth and arrived in the morning at the Castle of Loch Leven.

The Castle of Loch Leven is on a small island in the middle of the loch. It is nearly north from Edinburgh. The castle buildings covered at that time about one half of the island, the water coming up to the walls on three sides. On the other side was a little land, which was cultivated as a garden. The buildings inclosed a considerable area. There was a great square tower, marked on the plan below, which was the residence of the family. It consisted of four or five rooms, one over the other. The cellar, or, rather, what would be the cellar in other cases, was a dungeon for such prisoners as were to be kept in close confinement. The only entrance to this building was through a window in the second story, by means of a ladder which was raised and let down by a chain. This was over the point marked *e* on the plan. The chain was worked at a window in the story above. There were various other apartments and structures about the square, and among them there was a small octagonal tower in the corner at *m* which consisted within of one room over another for three stories, and a flat roof with battlements above. In the second story there was a window, *w*, looking upon the water. This was the only window having an external aspect in the whole fortress, all the other openings in the exterior walls being mere loop-holes and embrasures.

The following is a general plan of Loch Leven Castle:

MARY, QUEEN OF SCOTS

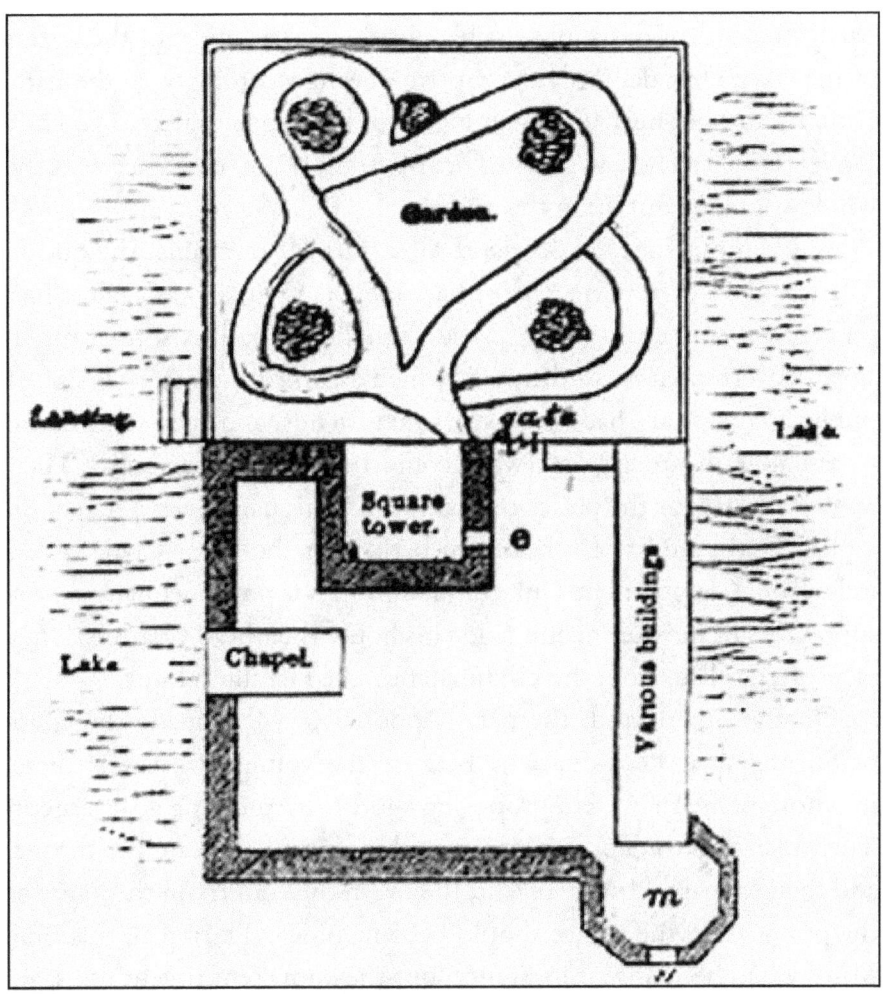

Plan of Loch Leven Castle

This castle was in possession of a certain personage styled the Lady Douglas. She was the mother of the Lord James, afterward the Earl of Murray, who has figured so conspicuously in this history as Mary's half brother, and at first her friend and counselor, though afterward her foe. Lady Douglas was commonly called the Lady of Loch Leven. She maintained that she had been lawfully married to James V., Mary's father, and that consequently her son, and not Mary, was the rightful heir to the crown. Of course she was Mary's natural enemy. They selected her castle as the place of Mary's confinement partly on this account, and

| 123 |

partly on account of its inaccessible position in the midst of the waters of the lake. They delivered the captive queen, accordingly, to the Lady Douglas and her husband, charging them to keep her safely. The Lady Douglas received her, and locked her up in the octagonal tower with the window looking out upon the water.

In the mean time, all Scotland took sides for or against the queen. The strongest party were against her; and the Church was against her, on account of their hostility to the Catholic religion. A sort of provisional government was instituted, which assumed the management of public affairs. Mary had, however, some friends, and they soon began to assemble in order to see what could be done for her cause. Their rendezvous was at the palace of Hamilton. This palace was situated on a plain in the midst of a beautiful park, near the River Clyde, a few miles from Glasgow. The Duke of Hamilton was prominent among the supporters of the queen, and made his house their head-quarters. They were often called, from this circumstance, the Hamilton lords.

On the other hand, the party opposed to Mary made the castle of Stirling their head-quarters, because the young prince was there, in whose name they were proposing soon to assume the government. Their plan was to depose Mary, or induce her to abdicate the throne, and then to make Murray regent, to govern the country in the name of the prince until the prince should become of age. During all this time Murray had been absent in France, but they now sent urgent messages to him to return. He obeyed the summons, and turned his face toward Scotland.

In the mean time, Mary continued in confinement in her little tower. She was not treated like a common prisoner, but had, in some degree, the attentions due to her rank. There were five or six female, and about as many male attendants; though, if the rooms which are exhibited to visitors at the present day as the apartments which she occupied are really such, her quarters were very contracted. They consist of small apartments of an octagonal form, one over the other, with tortuous and narrow stair-cases in the solid wall to ascend from one to the other. The roof and the floors of the tower are now gone, but the stair-ways, the capacious fire-places, the loop-holes, and the one window remain, enabling the visitor to reconstruct the dwelling in imagination, and even to fancy Mary herself there again, seated on the stone seat by the window, looking over the water at the distant hills, and sighing to be free.

The Hamilton lords were not strong enough to attempt her rescue. The weight of influence and power throughout the country went gradually and irresistibly into the other scale. There were great debates among the authorities of government as to what should be done. The Hamilton lords made proposals in behalf of Mary which the government could not accede to. Other proposals were made by different parties in the councils of the insurgent nobles, some more and some less hard for the captive queen. The conclusion, however, finally was, to urge Mary to resign her crown in favor of her son, and to appoint Murray, when he should return, to act as regent till the prince should be of age.

They accordingly sent commissioners to Loch Leven to propose these measures to the queen. There were three instruments of abdication prepared for her to sign. By one she resigned the crown in favor of her son. By the second she appointed Murray to be regent as soon as he should return from France. By the third she appointed commissioners to govern the country until Murray should return. They knew that Mary would be extremely unwilling to sign these papers, and yet that they must contrive, in some way, to obtain her signature without any open violence; for the signature, to be of legal force, must be, in some sense, her voluntary act.

The two commissioners whom they sent to her were Melville and Lindsay. Melville was a thoughtful and a reasonable man, who had long been in Mary's service, and who possessed a great share of her confidence and good will. Lindsay was, on the other hand, of an overbearing and violent temper, of very rude speech and demeanor, and was known to be unfriendly to the queen. They hoped that Mary would be induced to sign the papers by Melville's gentle persuasions; if not, Lindsay was to see what he could do by denunciations and threats.

When the two commissioners arrived at the castle, Melville alone went first into the presence of the queen. He opened the subject to her in a gentle and respectful manner. He laid before her the distracted state of Scotland, the uncertain and vague suspicions floating in the public mind on the subject of Darnley's murder, and the irretrievable shade which had been thrown over her position by the unhappy marriage with Bothwell; and he urged her to consent to the proposed measures, as the only way now left to restore peace to the land. Mary heard him patiently, but replied that she could not consent to his proposal. By doing so she should not only sacrifice her own rights, and degrade herself from the position she was entitled to occupy, but she should, in some sense, acknowledge herself guilty of the charges brought against her, and justify her enemies.

Melville, finding that his efforts were vain, called Lindsay in. He entered with a fierce and determined air. Mary was reminded of the terrible night when he and Ruthven broke into her little supper-room at Holyrood in quest of Rizzio. She was agitated and alarmed. Lindsay assailed her with denunciations and threats of the most violent character. There ensued a scene of the most rough and ferocious passion on the one side, and of anguish, terror, and despair on the other, which is said to have made this day the most wretched of all the wretched days of Mary's life. Sometimes she sat pale, motionless, and almost stupefied. At others, she was overwhelmed with sorrow and tears. She finally yielded; and, taking the pen, she signed the papers. Lindsay and Melville took them, left the castle gate, entered their boat, and were rowed away to the shore.

This was on the 25th of July, 1567, and four days afterward the young prince was crowned at Stirling. His title was James VI. Lindsay made oath at the coronation that he was a witness of Mary's abdication of the crown in favor of her son, and that it was her own free and voluntary act. James was about one year old. The coronation took place in the chapel where Mary had been crowned in her infancy, about twenty-five years before. Mary herself, though unconscious of her own coronation, mourned bitterly over that of her son. Unhappy mother! how little was she aware, when her heart was filled with joy and gladness at his birth, that in one short year his mere existence would furnish to her enemies the means of consummating and sealing her ruin.

On returning from the chapel to the state apartments of the castle, after the coronation, the noblemen by whom the infant had been crowned walked in solemn procession, bearing the badges and insignia of the newly-invested royalty. One carried the crown. Morton, who was to exercise the government until Murray should return, followed with the scepter, and a third bore the infant king, who gazed about unconsciously upon the scene, regardless alike of his mother's lonely wretchedness and of his own new scepter and crown.

In the mean time, Murray was drawing near toward the confines of Scotland. He was somewhat uncertain how to act. Having been absent for some time in France and on the Continent, he was not certain how far the people of Scotland were really and cordially in favor of the revolution which had been effected. Mary's friends might claim that her acts of abdication, having been obtained while she was under duress, were null and void, and if they were strong enough they might attempt to reinstate her upon the throne. In this case, it would be better for him not to have acted with the insurgent government at all. To gain information on these points, Murray sent to Melville to come and meet him on the border. Melville came. The result of their conferences was, that Murray resolved to visit Mary in her tower before he adopted any decisive course.

Murray accordingly journeyed northward to Loch Leven, and, embarking in the boat which plied between the castle and the shore, he crossed the sheet of water, and was admitted into the fortress. He had a long interview with Mary alone. At the sight of her long-absent brother, who had been her friend and guide in her early days of prosperity and happiness, and who had accompanied her through so many changing scenes, and who now returned, after his long separation from her, to find her a lonely and wretched captive, involved in irretrievable ruin, if not in acknowledged guilt, she was entirely overcome by her emotions. She burst into tears and could not speak. What further passed at this interview was never precisely known. They parted tolerably good friends, however, and yet Murray immediately assumed the government, by which it is supposed that he succeeded in persuading Mary that such a step was now best for her sake as well as for that of all others concerned.

Murray, however, did not fail to warn her, as he himself states, in a very serious manner, against any attempt to change her situation. "Madam," said he, "I will plainly declare to you what the sources of danger are from which I think you have most to apprehend. First, any attempt, of whatever kind, that you may make to create disturbance in the country, through friends that may still adhere to your cause, and to interfere with the government of your son; secondly, devising or attempting any plan of escape from this island; thirdly, taking any measures for inducing the Queen of England or the French king to come to your aid; and, lastly, persisting in your attachment to Earl Bothwell." He warned Mary solemnly against any and all of these, and then took his leave. He was soon after proclaimed regent. A Parliament was assembled to sanction all the proceedings, and the new government was established, apparently upon a firm foundation.

Mary remained, during the winter, in captivity, earnestly desiring, however, notwithstanding Murray's warning, to find some way of escape. She knew that there must be many who had remained friends to her cause. She thought that if she could once make her escape from her prison, these friends would rally around her, and that she could thus, perhaps, regain her throne again. But strictly watched as she was, and in a prison which was surrounded by the waters of a lake, all hope of escape seemed to be taken away.

Now there were, in the family of the Lord Douglas at the castle, two young men, George and William Douglas. The oldest, George, was about twenty-five years of age, and the youngest was seventeen. George was the son of Lord and Lady Douglas who kept the castle. William was an orphan boy, a relative, who, having no home, had been received into the family. These young men soon began to feel a strong interest in the beautiful captive confined in their father's castle, and, before many months, this interest became so strong that they began to feel willing to incur the dangers and responsibilities of aiding her in effecting her escape. They had secret conferences with Mary on the subject. They went to the shore on various pretexts, and contrived to make their plans known to Mary's friends, that they might be ready to receive her in case they should succeed.

The plan at length was ripe for execution. It was arranged thus. The castle not being large, there was not space within its walls for all the accommodations required for its inmates; much was done on the shore, where there was quite a little village of attendants and dependents pertaining to the castle. This little village has since grown into a flourishing manufacturing town, where a great variety of plaids, and tartans, and other Scotch fabrics are made. Its name is Kinross. Communication with this part of the shore was then, as now, kept up by boats, which generally then belonged to the castle, though now to the town.

On the day when Mary was to attempt her escape, a servant woman was brought by one of the castle boats from the shore with a bundle of clothes for Mary. Mary, whose health and strength had been impaired by her confinement and sufferings, was often in her bed. She was so at this time, though perhaps she was feigning now more feebleness than she really felt. The servant woman came into her apartment and undressed herself, while Mary rose, took the dress which she laid aside, and put it on as a disguise. The woman took Mary's place in bed. Mary covered her face with a muffler, and, taking another bundle in her hand to assist in her disguise, she passed across the court, issued from the castle gate, went to the landing stairs, and stepped into the boat for the men to row her to the shore.

The oarsmen, who belonged to the castle, supposing that all was right, pushed off, and began to row toward the land. As they were crossing the water, however, they observed that their passenger was very particular to keep her face covered, and attempted to pull away the muffler, saying, "Let us see what kind of a looking damsel this is." Mary, in alarm, put up her hands to her face to hold the muffler there. The smooth, white, and delicate fingers revealed to the men at once that they were carrying away a lady in disguise. Mary, finding that concealment was no longer possible, dropped her muffler, looked upon the men with composure and dignity, told them that she was their queen, that they were bound by their allegiance to her to obey her commands, and she commanded them to go on and row her to the shore.

The men decided, however, that their allegiance was due to the lord of the castle rather than to the helpless captive trying to escape from it. They told her that they must return. Mary was not only disappointed at the failure of her plans, but she was now anxious lest her friends, the young Douglases, should be implicated in the attempt, and should suffer in consequence of it. The men, however, solemnly promised her, that if she would quietly return, they would not make the circumstances known. The secret, however, was too great a secret to be kept. In a few days it all came to light. Lord and Lady Douglas were very angry with their son, and banished him, together with two of Mary's servants, from the castle. Whatever share young William Douglas had in the scheme was not found out, and he was suffered to remain. George Douglas went only to Kinross. He remained there watching for another opportunity to help Mary to her freedom.

Loch Leven Castle—The Place of Mary's Imprisonment

In the mean time, the watch and ward held over Mary was more strict and rigorous than ever, her keepers being resolved to double their vigilance, while George and William, on the other hand, resolved to redouble their exertions to find some means to circumvent it. William, who was only a boy of seventeen, and who remained within the castle, acted his part in a very sagacious and admirable manner. He was silent, and assumed a thoughtless and unconcerned manner in his general deportment, which put every one off their guard in respect to him. George, who was at Kinross, held frequent communications with the Hamilton lords, encouraging them to hope for Mary's escape, and leading them to continue in combination, and to be ready to act at a moment's warning. They communicated with each other, too, by secret means, across the lake, and with Mary in her solitary tower. It is said that George, wishing to make Mary understand that their plans for rescuing her were not abandoned, and not having the opportunity to do so directly, sent her a picture of the mouse liberating the lion from his snares, hoping that she would draw from the picture the inference which he intended.

At length the time arrived for another attempt. It was about the first of May. By looking at the engraving of Loch Leven Castle, it will be seen that there was a window in Mary's tower looking out over the water. George Douglas's plan was to bring a boat up to this window in the night, and take Mary down the wall into it. The place of egress by which Mary escaped is called in some of the accounts a postern gate, and yet tradition at the castle says that it was through this window. It is not improbable that this window might have been intended to be used sometimes as a postern gate, and that the iron grating with which it was guarded was made to open and shut, the key being kept with the other keys of the castle.

The time for the attempt was fixed upon for Sunday night, on the 2d of May. George Douglas was ready with the boat early in the evening. When it was dark, he rowed cautiously across the water, and took his position under Mary's window. William Douglas was in the mean time at supper in the great square tower with his father and mother. The keys were lying upon the table. He contrived to get them into his possession, and then cautiously stole away. He locked the tower as he came out, went across the court to Mary's room, liberated her through the postern window, and descended with her into the boat. One of her maids, whose name was Jane Kennedy, was to have accompanied her, but, in their eagerness to make sure of Mary, they forgot or neglected her, and she had to leap down after them, which feat she accomplished without any serious injury. The boat pushed off immediately, and the Douglases began to pull hard for the shore. They threw the keys of the castle into the lake, as if the impossibility of recovering them, in that case, made the imprisonment of the family more secure. The whole party were, of course, in the highest state of excitement and agitation. Jane Kennedy helped to row, and it is said that even Mary applied her strength to one of the oars.

They landed safely on the south side of the loch, far from Kinross. Several of the Hamilton lords were ready there to receive the fugitive. They mounted her on horseback, and galloped away. There was a strong party to escort her. They rode hard all night, and the next morning they arrived safely at Hamilton. "Now," said Mary, "I am once more a queen."

It was true. She was again a queen. Popular feeling ebbs and flows with prodigious force, and the change from one state to the other depends, sometimes, on very accidental causes. The news of Mary's escape spread rapidly over the land. Her friends were encouraged and emboldened. Sympathies, long dormant and inert, were awakened in her favor. She issued a proclamation, declaring that her abdication had been forced upon her, and, as such, was null and void. She summoned Murray to surrender his powers as regent, and to come and receive orders from her. She called upon all her faithful subjects to take up arms and gather around her standard. Murray refused to obey, but large masses of the people gave in their adhesion to their liberated queen, and flocked to Hamilton to enter into her service. In a week Mary found herself at the head of an army of six thousand men.

* * *

Ruins of Loch Leven Castle

The Castle of Loch Leven is now a solitary ruin. The waters of the loch have been lowered by means of an excavation of the outlet, and a portion of land has been left bare around the walls, which the proprietor has planted with trees. Visitors are taken from Kinross in a boat to view the scene. The square tower, though roofless and desolate, still stands. The window in the second story, which served as the entrance, and the one above, where the chain was worked, with the deep furrows in the sill cut by its friction, are shown by the guide. The court-yard is overgrown with weeds, and encumbered with fallen stones and old foundations. The chapel is gone, though its outline may be still traced in the ruins of its walls. The octagonal tower which Mary occupied remains, and the visitors, climbing up by the narrow stone stairs in the wall, look out at the window over the waters of the loch and the distant hills, and try to recreate in imagination the scene which the apartment presented when the unhappy captive was there.

# 11

## The Long Captivity

1568-1570

*Dumbarton Castle.—The situation and aspect.—Attempt to retreat to Dumbarton.—Mary's forces defeated.—Mary's flight.—Dundrennan. —Consultations.—Carlisle Castle.—Mary's message to the governor.— Lowther.—Mary's reception at the castle.—Is Mary a guest or a prisoner?—Precautions for guarding her.—Elizabeth's hypocrisy.—Dishonorable proposal.—Removal.—Separation from friends.—Proposed trial.— Opening of the court.—Adjourned to London.—Failure of the trial.— Mary's indignant pride.—Elizabeth's negotiations with Murray.—Their failure.—Cruel treatment of Lady Hamilton.—Hamilton resolves on revenge.—Hamilton's plans.—Death of Murray.—Hamilton's flight.— Mary's grief.—Duke of Norfolk beheaded.—Mary's unhappy situation. —Mary almost forgotten in her captivity.*

HAMILTON, which had been thus far the queen's place of rendezvous, was a palace rather than a castle, and therefore not a place of defense. It was situated, as has been already stated, on the River Clyde, *above* Glasgow; that is, toward the southeast of it, the River Clyde flowing toward the northwest. The Castle of Dumbarton, which has already been mentioned as the place from which Mary embarked for France in her early childhood, was below Glasgow, on the northern shore of the river. It stands there still in good repair, and is well garrisoned; it crowns a rock which rises abruptly from the midst of a comparatively level country, smiling with villages and cultivated fields, and frowns sternly upon the peaceful steamers and merchant ships which are continually gliding along under its guns, up and down the Clyde.

Queen Mary concluded to move forward to Dumbarton, it being a place of greater safety than Hamilton. Murray gathered his forces to intercept her march. The two armies met near Glasgow, as the queen was moving westward, down the river. There was a piece of rising ground between them, which each party was eager to ascend before the other should reach it. The leader of the forces on Murray's side ordered every horseman to take up a foot-soldier behind him, and ride with all speed to the top of the hill. By this means the great body of Murray's troops were put in possession of the vantage ground. The queen's forces took post on another rising ground, less favorable, at a little distance. The place was called Langside. A cannonading was soon commenced, and a general battle ensued. Mary watched the progress of it with intense emotions. Her forces began soon to give way, and before many hours they were retreating in all directions, the whole country being soon covered with the awful spectacles which are afforded by one terrified and panic-stricken army flying before the furious and triumphant rage of another. Mary gazed on the scene in an agony of grief and despair.

A few faithful friends kept near her side, and told her that she must hurry away. They turned to the southward, and rode away from the ground. They pressed on as rapidly as possible toward the southern coast, thinking that the only safety for Mary now was for her to make her escape from the country altogether, and go either to England or to France, in hopes of obtaining foreign aid to enable her to recover her throne. They at length reached the sea-coast. Mary was received into an abbey called Dundrennan, not far from the English frontier. Here she remained, with a few nobles and a small body of attendants, for two days, spending the time in anxious consultations to determine what should be done. Mary herself was in favor of going to England,

and appealing to Elizabeth for protection and help. Her friends and advisers, knowing Elizabeth perhaps better than Mary did, recommended that she should sail for France, in hopes of awakening sympathy there. But Mary, as we might naturally have expected, considering the circumstances under which she left that country, found herself extremely unwilling to go there as a fugitive and a suppliant. It was decided, finally, to go to England.

The nearest stronghold in England was Carlisle Castle, which was not very far from the frontier. The boundary between the two kingdoms is formed here by the Solway Frith, a broad arm of the sea. Dundrennan Abbey, to which Mary had retreated, was near the town of Kirkcudbright, which is, of course, on the northern side of the Frith; it is also near the sea. Carlisle is further up the Frith, near where the River Solway empties into it, and is twenty or thirty miles from the shore.

Mary sent a messenger to the governor of the castle at Carlisle to inquire whether he would receive and protect her. She could not, however, wait for an answer to this message, as the country was all in commotion, and she was exposed to an attack at any time from Murray's forces, in which case, even if they should not succeed in taking her captive, they might effectually cut off her retreat from Scottish ground. She accordingly determined to proceed immediately, and receive the answer from the governor of the castle on the way. She set out on the 16th of May. Eighteen or twenty persons constituted her train. This was all that remained to her of her army of six thousand men. She proceeded to the shore. They provided a fishing-boat for the voyage, furnishing it as comfortably for her as circumstances would admit. She embarked, and sailed along the coast, eastward, up the Frith, for about eighteen miles, gazing mournfully upon the receding shore of her native land—receding, in fact, now from her view forever. They landed at the most convenient port for reaching Carlisle, intending to take the remainder of the journey by land.

In the mean time, the messenger, on his arrival at Carlisle, found that the governor had gone to London. His second in rank, whom he had left in command, immediately sent off an express after him to inform him of the event. The name of this lieutenant-governor was Lowther. Lowther did all in Mary's favor that it was in his power to do. He directed the messenger to inform her that he had sent to London for instructions from Elizabeth, but that, in the mean time, she would be a welcome guest in his castle, and that he would defend her there from all her enemies. He then sent around to all the nobles and men of distinction in the neighborhood, informing them of the arrival of the distinguished visitor, and having assembled them, they proceeded together toward the coast to meet and receive the unhappy fugitive with the honors becoming her rank, though such honors must have seemed little else than a mockery in her present condition.

Mary was received at the castle as an honored guest. It is, however, a curious circumstance, that, in respect to the reception of princes and queens in royal castles, there is little or no distinction between the ceremonies which mark the honored guest and those which attend the helpless captive. Mary had a great many friends at first, who came out of Scotland to visit her. The authorities ordered repairs to be commenced upon the castle, to fit it more suitably for so distinguished an inmate, and, in consequence of the making of these repairs, they found it inconvenient to admit visitors. Of course, Mary, being a mere guest, could not complain. She wanted to take a walk beyond the limits of the castle, upon a green to which there was access through a postern gate. Certainly: the governor made no objection to such a walk, but sent twenty or thirty armed men to accompany her. They might be considered either as an honorary escort, or as a guard to watch her movements, to prevent her escape, and to secure her return. At one time she proposed to go a-hunting. They allowed her to go, *properly attended*. On her return, however, the officer reported to his superior that she was so admirable in her horsemanship, and could ride with so much fearlessness and speed, that he thought it might be possible for a body of her friends to come and carry her off, on some such occasion, back across the frontier. So they determined to tell Mary, when she wished to hunt again, that they thought it not safe for her to go out on such excursions, as her *enemies* might make a sudden invasion and carry her away. The precautions would be just the same to protect Mary from her enemies as to keep her from her friends.

Elizabeth sent her captive cousin very kind and condoling messages, dispatching, however, by the same messenger stringent orders to the commander of the castle to be sure and keep her safely. Mary asked for an interview with Elizabeth. Elizabeth's officers replied that she could not properly admit Mary to a personal interview until she had been, in some way or other, cleared of the suspicion which attached to her in respect to the murder of Darnley. They proposed, moreover, that Mary should consent to have that question examined before some sort of court which Elizabeth might constitute for this purpose. Now it is a special point of honor among all sovereign kings and queens, throughout the civilized world, that they can, technically, do no wrong; that they can not in any way be brought to trial; and especially that they can not be, by any means or in any way, amenable to each other. Mary refused to acknowledge any English jurisdiction whatever in respect to any charges brought against her, a sovereign queen of Scotland.

Elizabeth removed her prisoner to another castle further from the frontier than Carlisle, in order to place her in a situation where she would be more safe *from her enemies*. It was not convenient to lodge so many of her attendants at these new quarters as in the other fortress, and several were dismissed. Additional obstructions were thrown in the way of her seeing friends and visitors from Scotland. Mary found her situation growing every day more and more helpless and desolate. Elizabeth urged continually upon her the necessity of having the points at issue between herself and Murray examined by a commissioner, artfully putting it on the ground, not of a trial of Mary, but a calling of Murray to account, by Mary, for his usurpation. At last, harassed and worn down, and finding no ray of hope coming to her from any quarter, she consented. Elizabeth constituted such a court, which was to meet at York, a large and ancient city in the north of England. Murray was to appear there in person, with other lords associated with him. Mary appointed commissioners to appear for her; and the two parties went into court, each thinking that it was the other which was accused and on trial.

The court assembled, and, after being opened with great parade and ceremony, commenced the investigation of the questions at issue, which led, of course, to endless criminations and recriminations, the ground covering the whole history of Mary's career in Scotland. They went on for some weeks in this hopeless labyrinth, until, at length, Murray produced the famous letters alleged to have been written by Mary to Bothwell before Darnley's murder, as a part of the evidence, and charged Mary, on the strength of this evidence, with having been an abettor in the murder. Elizabeth, finding that the affair was becoming, as in fact she wished it to become, more and more involved, and wishing to get Mary more and more entangled in it, and to draw her still further into her power, ordered the conference, as the court was called, to be adjourned to London. Here things took such a turn that Mary complained that she was herself treated in so unjust a manner, and Murray and his cause were allowed so many unfair advantages, that she could not allow the discussion on her part to continue. The conference was accordingly broken up, each party charging the other with being the cause of the interruption.

Murray returned to Scotland to resume his government there. Mary was held a closer captive than ever. She sent to Elizabeth asking her to remove these restraints, and allow her to depart either to her own country or to France. Elizabeth replied that she could not, considering all the circumstances of the case, allow her to leave England; but that, if she would give up all claims to the government of Scotland to her son, the young prince, she might remain in peace *in* England. Mary replied that she would suffer death a thousand times rather than dishonor herself in the eyes of the world by abandoning, in such a way, her rights as a sovereign. The last words which she should speak, she said, should be those of the Queen of Scotland.

Elizabeth therefore considered that she had no alternative left but to keep Mary a prisoner. She accordingly retained her for some time in confinement, but she soon found that such a charge was a serious incumbrance to her, and one not unattended with danger. The disaffected in her own realm were beginning to form plots, and to consider whether they could not, in some way or other, make use of Mary's claims to the English crown to aid them. Finally, Elizabeth came to the conclusion, when she had become a little satiated with the feeling, at first so delightful, of having Mary in her power, that, after all, it would be quite as convenient to have her imprisoned in Scotland, and she opened a negotiation with Murray for delivering Mary into his hands. He was, on his part, to agree to save her life, and to keep her a close prisoner, and he was to deliver hostages to Elizabeth as security for the fulfillment of these obligations.

Various difficulties, however, occurred in the way of the accomplishment of these plans, and before the arrangement was finally completed, it was cut suddenly short by Murray's miserable end. One of the Hamiltons, who had been with Mary at Langside, was taken prisoner after the battle. Murray, who, of course, as the legally constituted regent in the name of James, considered himself as representing the royal authority of the kingdom, regarded these prisoners as rebels taken in the act of insurrection against their sovereign. They were condemned to death, but finally were pardoned at the place of execution. Their estates were, however, confiscated, and given to the followers and favorites of Murray.

One of these men, in taking possession of the house of Hamilton, with a cruel brutality characteristic of the times, turned Hamilton's family out abruptly in a cold night—perhaps exasperated by resistance which he may have encountered. The wife of Hamilton, it is said, was sent out naked; but the expression means, probably, very insufficiently clothed for such an exposure. At any rate, the unhappy outcast wandered about, half frantic with anger and terror, until, before morning, she was wholly frantic and insane. To have such a calamity brought upon him in consequence merely of his fidelity to his queen, was, as the bereaved and wretched husband thought, an injury not to be borne. He considered Murray the responsible author of these miseries, and silently and calmly resolved on a terrible revenge.

Murray was making a progress through the country, traveling in state with a great retinue, and was to pass through Linlithgow. There is a town of that name close by the palace. Hamilton provided himself with a room in one of the houses on the principal street, through which he knew that Murray must pass. He had a fleet horse ready for him at the back door. The front door was barricaded. There was a sort of balcony or gallery projecting toward the street, with a window in it. He stationed himself here, having carefully taken every precaution to prevent his being seen from the street, or overheard in his movements. Murray lodged in the town during the night, and Hamilton posted himself in his ambuscade the next morning, armed with a gun.

The town was thronged, and Murray, on issuing from his lodging, escorted by his cavalcade, found the streets crowded with spectators. He made his way slowly, on account of the throng. When he arrived at the proper point, Hamilton took his aim in a cool and deliberate manner, screened from observation by black cloths with which he had darkened his hiding-place. He fired. The ball passed through the body of the regent, and thence, descending as it went, killed a horse on the other side of him. Murray fell. There was a universal outcry of surprise and fear. They made an onset upon the house from which the shot had been fired. The door was strongly barricaded. Before they could get the means to force an entrance, Hamilton was on his horse and far away. The regent was carried to his lodgings, and died that night.

Murray was Queen Mary's half brother, and the connection of his fortunes with hers, considered in respect to its intimacy and the length of its duration, was, on the whole, greater than that of any other individual. He may be said to have governed Scotland, in reality, during the whole of Mary's nominal reign, first as her minister and friend, and afterward as her competitor and foe. He was, at any rate, during most of her life, her nearest relative and her most constant companion, and Mary mourned his death with many tears.

There was a great nobleman in England, named the Duke of Norfolk, who had vast estates, and was regarded as the greatest subject in the realm. He was a Catholic. Among the other countless schemes and plots to which Mary's presence in England gave rise, he formed a plan of marrying her, and, through her claim to the crown and by the help of the Catholics, to overturn the government of Elizabeth. He entered into negotiations with Mary, and she consented to become his wife, without, however, as she says, being a party to his political schemes. His plots were discovered; he was imprisoned, tried, and beheaded. Mary was accused of sharing the guilt of his treason. She denied this. She was not very vigorously proceeded against, but she suffered in the event of the affair another sad disappointment of her hopes of liberty, and her confinement became more strict and absolute than ever.

Still she had quite a numerous retinue of attendants. Many of her former friends were allowed to continue with her. Jane Kennedy, who had escaped with her from Loch Leven, remained in her service. She was removed from castle to castle, at Elizabeth's orders, to diminish the probability of the forming and maturing of plans of escape. She amused herself sometimes in embroidery and similar pursuits, and sometimes she pined and languished under the pressure of her sorrows and woes. Sixteen or eighteen years passed away in this manner. She was almost forgotten. Very exciting public events were taking place in England and in Scotland, and the name of the poor captive queen at length seemed to pass from men's minds, except so far as it was whispered secretly in plots and intrigues.

# 12

# The End

### 1586-1587

*Plots and intrigues.—How far Mary was involved.—Babington's conspiracy.—Secret correspondence.—Seizure of Mary's papers.—Her son James. —Elizabeth resolves to bring Mary to trial.—Fotheringay Castle.—Great interest in the trial.—Preparations for it.—The throne.—Mary refuses to plead.—The commission.—The great hall.—Mary pronounced guilty.— Elizabeth's pretended sorrow.—Signing the warrant.—Shuffling of Elizabeth.—Mary's letter to Elizabeth.—Interposition of Mary's friends.— Elizabeth signs the warrant.—It is read to Mary.—Mary hears the sentence with composure.—Protests her innocence.—Mary refused a priest.— Mary alone with her friends.—Affecting scene.—Supper.—Mary's farewell to her attendants.—Mary's last letters.—Her directions as to the disposal of her body.—Arrangements for the execution.—The scaffold.— Proceeding to the hall.—Interview with Melville.—Mary's last message. —She desires the presence of her attendants.—Mary's dress and appearance.—Symbols of religion.—Mary's firmness in her faith.—Her last prayer.—The execution.—Heart-rending scene.—Disposition of the body. —Elizabeth's affected surprise.—Her conduct.—The end of Mary's ambition realized.—Accession of James I.—Tomb of Mary at Westminster Abbey.—Mary's love and ambition.—She triumphs in the end.*

MARY did not always discourage the plots and intrigues with which her name was connected. She, of course, longed for deliverance from the thraldom in which Elizabeth held her, and was ready to embrace any opportunity which promised release. She thus seems to have listened from time to time to the overtures which were made to her, and involved herself, in Elizabeth's opinion, more or less, in the responsibility which attached to them. Elizabeth did not, however, in such cases, do any thing more than to increase somewhat the rigors of her imprisonment. She was afraid to proceed to extremities with her, partly, perhaps, for fear that she might, by doing so, awaken the hostility of France, whose king was Mary's cousin, or of Scotland, whose monarch was her son.

At length, however, in the year 1586, about eighteen years from the commencement of Mary's captivity, a plot was formed in which she became so seriously involved as to subject herself to the charge of aiding and abetting in the high treason of which the leaders of the plot were proved to be guilty. This plot is known in history by the name of Babington's conspiracy. Babington was a young gentleman of fortune, who lived in the heart of England. He was inspired with a strong degree of interest in Mary's fate, and wished to rescue her from her captivity. He joined himself with a large party of influential individuals of the Catholic faith. The conspirators opened negotiations with the courts of France and Spain for aid. They planned an insurrection, the assassination of Elizabeth, the rescue of Mary, and a general revolution. They maintained a correspondence with Mary. This correspondence was managed very secretly, the letters being placed by a confidential messenger in a certain hole in the castle wall where Queen Mary was confined.

One day, when Mary was going out to ride, just as she was entering her carriage, officers suddenly arrived from London. They told her that the plot in which she had been engaged had been discovered; that fourteen of the principal conspirators had been hung, seven on each of two successive days, and that they had come to arrest some of her attendants and to seize her papers. They accordingly went into her apartments, opened all her desks, trunks, and cabinets, seized her papers, and took them to London. Mary sat down in the scene of desolation and disorder which they left, and wept bitterly.

The papers which were seized were taken to London, and Elizabeth's government began seriously to agitate the question of bringing Mary herself to trial. One would have thought that, in her forlorn and desolate condition, she would have looked to her son for sympathy and aid. But rival claimants to a crown can have little kind feeling to each other, even if they are mother and son. James, as he gradually approached toward maturity, took sides against his mother. In fact, all Scotland was divided, and was for many years in a state of civil war: those who advocated Mary's right to the crown on one side, and James's adherents on the other. They were called king's men and queen's men. James was, of course, brought up in hostility to his mother, and he wrote to her, about a year before Babington's conspiracy, in terms so hostile and so devoid of filial love, that his ingratitude stung her to the heart. "Was it for this," she said, "that I made so many sacrifices, and endured so many trials on his account in his early years? I have made it the whole business of my life to protect and secure his rights, and to open before him a prospect of future power and glory: and this is the return."

The English government, under Elizabeth's direction, concluded to bring Mary to a public trial. They removed her, accordingly, to the Castle of Fotheringay. Fotheringay is in Northamptonshire, which is in the very heart of England, Northampton, the shire town, being about sixty miles northwest of London. Fotheringay Castle was on the banks of the River Nen, or Avon, which flows northeast from Northampton to the sea. A few miles below the castle is the ancient town of Peterborough, where there was a monastery and a great cathedral church. The monastery had been built a thousand years before.

They removed Mary to Fotheringay Castle for her trial, and lawyers, counselors, commissioners, and officers of state began to assemble there from all quarters. The castle was a spacious structure. It was surrounded with two moats, and with double walls, and was strongly fortified. It contained numerous and spacious apartments, and it had especially one large hall which was well adapted to the purposes of this great trial. The preparations for the solemn ordeal through which Mary was now to pass, brought her forth from the obscurity in which she had so long been lost to the eyes of mankind, and made her the universal object of interest and attention in England, Scotland, and France. The people of all these nations looked on with great interest at the spectacle of one queen tried solemnly on a charge of high treason against another. The stories of her beauty, her graces, her misfortunes, which had slumbered for eighteen years, were all now revived, and every body felt a warm interest in the poor captive, worn down by long confinement, and trembling in the hands of what they feared would be a merciless and terrible power.

Mary was removed to the Castle of Fotheringay toward the end of September, 1586. The preparations for the trial proceeded slowly. Every thing in which kings and queens, or affairs of state were concerned in those days, was conducted with great pomp and ceremony. The arrangements of the hall were minutely prescribed. At the head of it a sort of throne was placed, with a royal canopy over it, for the Queen of England. This, though it was vacant, impressed the court and the spectators as a symbol of royalty, and denoted that the sovereignty of Elizabeth was the power before which Mary was arraigned.

When the preparations were made, Mary refused to acknowledge the jurisdiction of the court. She denied that they had any right to arraign or to try her. "I am no subject of Elizabeth's," said she. "I am an independent and sovereign queen as well as she, and I will not consent to any thing inconsistent with this my true position. I owe no allegiance to England, and I am not, in any sense, subject to her laws. I came into the realm only to ask assistance from a sister queen, and I have been made a captive, and detained many years in an unjust and cruel imprisonment; and though now worn down both in body and mind by my protracted sufferings, I am not yet so enfeebled as to forget what is due to myself, my ancestors, and my country."

This refusal of Mary's to plead, or to acknowledge the jurisdiction of the court, caused a new delay. They urged her to abandon her resolution. They told her that if she refused to plead, the trial would proceed without her action, and, by pursuing such a course, she would only deprive herself of the means of defense, without at all impeding the course of her fate. At length Mary yielded. It would have been better for her to have adhered to her first intention.

The commission by which Mary was to be tried consisted of earls, barons, and other persons of rank, twenty or thirty in number. They were seated on each side of the room, the throne being at the head. In the center was a table, where the lawyers, by whom the trial was to be conducted, were seated. Below this table was a chair for Mary. Behind Mary's chair was a rail, dividing off the lower end of the hall from the court; and this formed an outer space, to which some spectators were admitted.

Mary took her place in the seat assigned her, and the trial proceeded. They adduced the evidence against her, and then asked for her defense. She said substantially that she had a right to make an effort to recover her liberty; that, after being confined a captive so long, and having lost forever her youth, her health, and her happiness, it was not wonderful that she wished to be free; but that, in endeavoring to obtain her freedom, she had formed no plans to injure Elizabeth, or to interfere in any way with her rights or prerogatives as queen. The commissioners, after devoting some days to hearing evidence, and listening to the defense, sent Mary back to her apartments, and went to London. There they had a final consultation, and unanimously agreed in the following decision: "That Mary, commonly called Queen of Scots and dowager of France, had been an accessory to Babington's conspiracy, and had compassed the death of Elizabeth, queen of England."

Elizabeth pretended to be very much concerned at this result. She laid the proceedings before Parliament. It was supposed then, and has always been supposed since, that she wished Mary to be beheaded, but desired not to take the responsibility of it herself; and that she wanted to appear unwilling, and to be impelled, greatly against her own inclinations, by the urgency of others, to carry the sentence into execution. At any rate, Parliament, and all the members of the government, approved and confirmed the verdict, and wished to have it carried into effect.

It has always been the custom, in modern times, to require the solemn act of the supreme magistrate of any state to confirm a decision of a tribunal which condemns a person to death, by signing what is called a warrant for the execution. This is done by the king or queen in England, and by the governor in one of the United States. This warrant is an order, very formally written, and sealed with the great seal, authorizing the executioner to proceed, and carry the sentence into effect. Of course, Queen Mary could not be executed unless Elizabeth should first sign the warrant. Elizabeth would herself, probably, have been better pleased to have been excused from all direct agency in the affair. But this could not be. She, however, made much delay, and affected great unwillingness to proceed. She sent messengers to Mary, telling her what the sentence had been, how sorry she was to hear it, and how much she desired to save her life, if it were possible. At the same time, she told her that she feared it might not be in her power, and she advised Mary to prepare her mind for the execution of the sentence.

Mary wrote a letter to Elizabeth in reply. She said in this letter that she was glad to hear that they had pronounced sentence of death against her, for she was weary of life, and had no hope of relief or rest from her miseries but in the grave. She wrote, therefore, not to ask any change in the decision, but to make three requests. First, that, after her execution, her body might be removed to France, and be deposited at Rheims, where the ashes of her mother were reposing. Secondly, that her execution should not be in secret, but that her personal friends might be present, to attest to the world that she met her fate with resignation and fortitude; and, thirdly, that her attendants and friends, who had, through their faithful love for her, shared her captivity so long, might be permitted to retire wherever they pleased, after her death, without any molestation. "I hope," said she, in conclusion, "you will not refuse me these my dying requests, but that you will assure me by a letter under your own hand that you will comply with them, and then I shall die as I have lived, your affectionate sister and prisoner, Mary Queen of Scots."

The King of France, and James, Mary's son in Scotland, made somewhat vigorous efforts to arrest the execution of the sentence which had been pronounced against Mary. From these and other causes, the signing of the warrant was delayed for some months, but at length Elizabeth yielded to the solicitations of her ministers. She affixed her signature to the instrument. The chancellor put upon it the great seal, and the commissioners who were appointed by it to superintend the execution went to Fotheringay. They arrived there on the 7th of February, 1587.

After resting, and refreshing themselves for a short time from their journey, the commissioners sent word to Mary that they wished for an interview with her. Mary had retired. They said that their business was very important. She rose, and prepared to receive them. She assembled all her attendants, fourteen or fifteen in number, in order to receive the commissioners in a manner comporting, so far as circumstances allowed, with her rank and station. The commissioners were at length ushered into the apartment. They stood respectfully before her, with their heads uncovered. The foremost then, in language as forbearing and gentle as was consistent with the nature of his message, informed her that it had been decided to carry the sentence which had been pronounced against her into effect, and then he requested another of the number to read the warrant for her execution.

Fotheringay Castle in Former Times

Mary listened to it calmly and patiently. Her attendants, one after another, were overcome by the mournful and awful solemnity of the scene, and melted into tears. Mary, however, was calm. When the reading of the warrant was ended, she said that she was sorry that her cousin Elizabeth should set the example of taking the life of a sovereign queen; but for herself, she was willing to die. Life had long ceased to afford her any peace or happiness, and she was ready to exchange it for the prospect of immortality. She then laid her hand upon the New Testament, which was near her, of course a Catholic version, and called God to witness that she had never plotted herself, or joined in plots with others, for the death of Elizabeth. One of the commissioners remarked that her oath being upon a Catholic version of the Bible, they should not consider it valid. She rejoined that it ought to be considered the more sacred and solemn on that account, as that was the version which she regarded as the only one which was authoritative and true.

Mary then asked the commissioners several questions, as whether her son James had not expressed any interest in her fate, and whether no foreign princes had interposed to save her. The commissioners answered these and other inquiries, and Mary learned from their answers that her fate was sealed. She then asked them what time was appointed for the execution. They replied that it was to take place at eight o'clock the following morning.

Mary had not expected so early an hour to be named. She said it was sudden; and she seemed agitated and distressed. She, however, soon recovered her composure, and asked to have a Catholic priest allowed to visit her. The commissioners replied that that could not be permitted. They, however, proposed to send the Dean of Peterborough to visit her. A dean is the ecclesiastical functionary presiding over a cathedral church; and, of course, the Dean of Peterborough was the clergyman of the highest rank in that vicinity. He was, however, a Protestant, and Mary did not wish to see him.

The commissioners withdrew, and left Mary with her friends, when there ensued one of those scenes of anguish and suffering which those who witness them never forget, but carry the gloomy remembrance of them, like a dark shadow in the soul, to the end of their days. Mary was quiet, and appeared calm. It may however, have been the calm of hopeless and absolute despair. Her attendants were overwhelmed with agitation and grief, the expression of which they could not even attempt to control. At last they became more composed, and Mary asked them to kneel with her in prayer; and she prayed for some time fervently and earnestly in the midst of them.

She then directed supper to be prepared as usual, and, until it was ready, she spent her time in dividing the money which she had on hand into separate parcels for her attendants, marking each parcel with the name. She sat down at the table when supper was served, and though she ate but little, she conversed as usual, in a cheerful manner, and with smiles. Her friends were silent and sad, struggling continually to keep back their tears. At the close of the supper Mary called for a cup of wine, and drank to the health of each one of them, and then asked them to drink to her. They took the cup, and, kneeling before her, complied with her request, though, as they did it, the tears would come to their eyes. Mary then told them that she willingly forgave them for all that they had ever done to displease her, and she thanked them for their long-continued fidelity and love. She also asked that they would forgive her for any thing she might ever have done in respect to them which was inconsistent with her duty. They answered the request only with a renewal of their tears.

Mary spent the evening in writing two letters to her nearest relatives in France, and in making her will. The principal object of these letters was to recommend her servants to the attention and care of those to whom they were addressed, after she should be gone. She went to bed shortly after midnight, and it is said she slept. This would be incredible, if any thing were incredible in respect to the workings of the human soul in a time of awful trial like this, which so transcends all the ordinary conditions of its existence.

At any rate, whether Mary slept or not, the morning soon came. Her friends were around her as soon as she rose. She gave them minute directions about the disposition of her body. She wished to have it taken to France to be interred, as she had requested of Elizabeth, either at Rheims, in the same tomb with the body of her mother, or else at St. Denis, an ancient abbey a little north of Paris, where the ashes of a long line of French monarchs repose. She begged her servants, if possible, not to leave her body till it should reach its final home in one of these places of sepulture.

In the mean time, arrangements had been made for the last act in this dreadful tragedy, in the same great hall where she had been tried. They raised a platform upon the stone floor of the hall large enough to contain those who were to take part in the closing scene. On this platform was a block, a cushion, and a chair. All these things, as well as the platform itself, were covered with black cloth, giving to the whole scene a most solemn and funereal expression. The part of the hall containing this scaffold was railed off from the rest. The governor of the castle, and a body of guards, came in and took their station at the sides of the room. Two executioners, one holding the axe, stood upon the scaffold on one side of the block. Two of the commissioners stood upon the other side. The remaining commissioners and several gentlemen of the neighborhood took their places as spectators without the rail. The number of persons thus assembled was about two hundred. Strange that any one should have come in, voluntarily, to witness such a scene!

When all was ready, the sheriff, carrying his white wand of office, and attended by some of the commissioners, went for Mary. She was at her devotions, and she asked a little delay that she might conclude them: perhaps the shrinking spirit clung at the last moment to life, and wished to linger a few minutes longer before taking the final farewell. The request was granted. In a short time Mary signified that she was ready, and they began to move toward the hall of execution. Her attendants were going to accompany her. The sheriff said this could not be allowed. She accordingly bade them farewell, and they filled the castle with the sound of their shrieks and lamentations.

Mary went on, descending the stair-case, at the foot of which she was joined by one of her attendants, from whom she had been separated for some time. His name was Sir Andrew Melville, and he was the master of her household. The name of her secretary Melville was James. Sir Andrew kneeled before her, kissed her hand, and said that this was the saddest hour of his life. Mary began to give him some last commissions and requests. "Say," said she, "that I died firm in the faith; that I forgive my enemies; that I feel that I have never disgraced Scotland, my native country, and that I have been always true to France, the land of my happiest years. Tell my son—" Here her voice faltered and ceased to be heard, and she burst into tears.

She struggled to regain her composure. "Tell my son," said she, "that I thought of him in my last moments, and that I have never yielded, either by word or deed, to any thing whatever that might lead to his prejudice. Tell him to cherish the memory of his mother, and say that I sincerely hope his life may be happier than mine has been."

Mary then turned to the commissioners who stood by, and renewed her request that her attendants, who had just been separated from her, might come down and see her die. The commissioners objected. They said that if these attendants were admitted, their anguish and lamentations would only add to her own distress, and make the whole scene more painful. Mary, however, urged the request. She said they had been devotedly attached to her all her days; they had shared her captivity, and loved and served her faithfully to the end, and it was enough if she herself, and they, desired that they should be present. The commissioners at last yielded, and allowed her to name six, who should be summoned to attend her. She did so, and the six came down.

The sad procession then proceeded to the hall. Mary was in full court dress, and walked into the apartment with the air and composure of a reigning queen. She leaned on the arm of her physician. Sir Andrew Melville followed, bearing the train of her robe. Her dress is described as a gown of black silk, bordered with crimson velvet, over which was a satin mantle. A long veil of white crape, edged with rich lace, hung down almost to the ground. Around her neck was an ivory crucifix—that is, an image of Christ upon the cross, which the Catholics use as a memorial of our Savior's sufferings—and a rosary, which is a string of beads of peculiar arrangement, often employed by them as an aid in their devotions. Mary meant, doubtless, by these symbols, to show to her enemies and to the world, that though she submitted to her fate without resistance, yet, so far as the contest of her life had been one of religious faith, she had no intention of yielding.

Mary ascended the platform and took her seat in the chair provided for her. With the exception of stifled sobs here and there to be heard, the room was still. An officer then advanced and read the warrant of execution, which the executioners listened to as their authority for doing the dreadful work which they were about to perform. The Dean of Peterborough, the Protestant ecclesiastic whom Mary had refused to see, then came forward to the foot of the platform, and most absurdly commenced an address to her, with a view to convert her to the Protestant faith. Mary interrupted him, saying that she had been born and had lived a Catholic, and she was resolved so to die; and she asked him to spare her his useless reasonings. The dean persisted in going on. Mary turned away from him, kneeled down, and began to offer a Latin prayer. The dean soon brought his ministrations to a close, and then Mary prayed for some time, in a distinct and fervent voice, in English, the large company listening with breathless attention. She prayed for her own soul, and that she might have comfort from heaven in the agony of death. She implored God's blessing upon France; upon Scotland; upon England; upon Queen Elizabeth; and, more than all, upon her son. During this time she held the ivory crucifix in her hand, clasping it and raising it from time to time toward heaven.

When her prayer was ended, she rose, and, with the assistance of her attendants, took off her veil, and such other parts of her dress as it was necessary to remove in order to leave the neck bare, and then she kneeled forward and laid her head upon the block. The agitation of the assembly became extreme. Some turned away from the scene faint and sick at heart; some looked more eagerly and intensely at the group upon the scaffold; some wept and sobbed aloud. The assistant executioner put Mary's two hands together and held them; the other raised his axe, and, after the horrid sound of two or three successive blows, the assistant held up the dissevered head, saying, "So perish all Queen Elizabeth's enemies."

The assembly dispersed. The body was taken into an adjoining apartment, and prepared for interment. Mary's attendants wished to have it delivered to them, that they might comply with her dying request to convey it to France; but they were told that they could not be allowed to do so. The body was interred with great pomp and ceremony in the Cathedral at Peterborough, where it remained in peace for many years.

\* \* \*

Now that the deed was done, the great problem with Elizabeth was, of course, to avert the consequences of the terrible displeasure and thirst for revenge which she might naturally suppose it would awaken in Scotland and in France. She succeeded very well in accomplishing this.

As soon as she heard of the execution of Mary, she expressed the utmost surprise, grief, and indignation. She said that she had, indeed, signed the death warrant, but it was not her intention at all to have it executed; and that, when she delivered it to the officer, she charged him not to let it go out of his possession. This the officer denied. Elizabeth insisted, and punished the officer by a long imprisonment, and perpetual disgrace, for his pretended offense. She sent a messenger to James, explaining the terrible accident, as she termed it, which had occurred, and deprecating his displeasure. James, though at first filled with indignation, and determined to avenge his mother's death, allowed himself to be appeased.

About twenty years after this, Elizabeth died, and the great object of Mary's ambition throughout her whole life was attained by the union of the Scotch and English crowns on the head of her son. As soon as Elizabeth ceased to breathe, James the Sixth of Scotland was proclaimed James the First of England. He was at that time nearly forty years of age. He was married, and had several young children. The circumstances of King James's journey to London, when he went to take possession of his new kingdom, are related in the History of Charles I., belonging to this series. Though James thus became monarch of both England and Scotland, it must not be supposed that the two *kingdoms* were combined. They remained separate for many years—two independent kingdoms governed by one king.

When James succeeded to the English throne, his mother had been dead many years, and whatever feelings of affection may have bound his heart to her in early life, they were now well-nigh obliterated by the lapse of time, and by the new ties by which he was connected with his wife and his children. As soon as he was seated on his new throne, however, he ordered the Castle of Fotheringay, which had been the scene of his mother's trial and death, to be leveled with the ground, and he transferred her remains to Westminster Abbey, where they still repose.

Mary's Tomb in Westminster Abbey

If the lifeless dust had retained its consciousness when it was thus transferred, with what intense emotions of pride and pleasure would the mother's heart have been filled, in being thus brought to her final home in that ancient sepulcher of the English kings, by her son, now, at last, safely established, where she had so long toiled and suffered to instate him, in his place in the line. Ambition was the great, paramount, ruling principle of Mary's life.

Love was, with her, an occasional, though perfectly uncontrollable impulse, which came suddenly to interrupt her plans and divert her from her course, leaving her to get back to it again, after devious wanderings, with great difficulty and through many tears. The love, with the consequences which followed from it, destroyed *her*; while the ambition, recovering itself after every contest with its rival, and holding out perseveringly to the last, saved *her son*; so that, in the long contest in which her life was spent, though she suffered all the way, and at last sacrificed herself, she triumphed in the end.

## THE END

# ABOUT JACOB ABBOTT

Jacob Abbott was born in Hallowell, Maine in 1803, the son of a minister and farmer. Even as a young boy, he showed academic promise and an interest in spiritual matters. After attending the Hallowell Academy, he was admitted to Bowdoin College at the age of 14.

At Bowdoin, Abbott studied classics and mathematics. He graduated second in his class in 1820 at the young age of 16. He was known as a serious and studious young man who strove for excellence.

After college, Abbott went on to study at Andover Theological Seminary with the intention of becoming a Congregationalist minister. However, his rigorous study habits and frail health caused him to abandon this pursuit after just two years.

Abbott was plagued by gastrointestinal issues and migraines throughout his life, likely exacerbated by the demanding academic environment. His poor health finally forced him to leave his ministerial studies and turn to the less stressful pursuits of writing and tutoring.

First, Abbott took a job as a professor of mathematics and natural philosophy at Amherst College in 1824. The following year, he married Harriet Vaughan and moved to Boston where he opened a school for young ladies. It was during this time that he began writing simple textbooks for teaching science, history and Christian values.

So while Abbott had aspired to be a minister, chronic health issues led him to find an alternate calling educating children through clear and engaging writing. This pivot would launch his successful career as one of the most famous children's authors of the 19th century.

In 1825, Abbott married Harriet Vaughan and soon after started his own school for young ladies in Boston. During this time, he began

## ABOUT JACOB ABBOTT

writing educational books in a popular, simple style. His early works included the Mount Vernon Reader and The Young Christian.

Abbott gained fame with the Rollo series, first published in 1835. These stories followed a young boy named Rollo learning morals and virtues through his everyday adventures. The series was hugely popular and established Abbott's reputation as a gifted children's writer.

Other notable books by Abbott include the Franconia Stories (1853-1873), a 10-volume series about a brother and sister's adventures in the country, and the Marco Paul series (1853-1873), which followed a boy's travels around America learning about each state.

In all, Jacob Abbott wrote over 200 books, primarily for young readers. His works were praised for their ability to educate and impart moral lessons in an engaging, story-driven way. Though largely forgotten today, he was one of the most prolific and beloved children's authors of his era.

Abbott continued writing up until his death on October 31, 1879 in Farmington, Maine. His legacy lives on through his contributions to 19th century children's literature.

# BIOGRAPHIES ABBOTT WROTE

A number of the books Abbott wrote were biographies of famous people. Famous characters covered in these books included:

**Alexander the Great:** This book provides a sweeping look at the life and achievements of Alexander III of Macedon, better known as Alexander the Great. It follows his early education by Aristotle, ascension to the throne after his father Philip II's assassination, and extensive military campaigns across Asia and northeast Africa. Abbott recounts Alexander's major battles against the Persians and annexation of their empire. The book also examines Alexander's tactics, military innovations, and creation of a Hellenistic empire stretching from Greece to India before his death at 32.

**Alfred the Great:** This biography focuses on Alfred's defense of the Kingdom of Wessex against Viking raids in 9th century England. It discusses how Alfred drove back the Great Heathen Army and then negotiated terms with the Vikings, designating parts of England for their settlement. Abbott also highlights Alfred's efforts to revive learning and education in England, as well as his codification of laws and strengthening of the Anglo-Saxon navy. The book frames Alfred as a scholarly, strategic and devout ruler whose achievements laid the foundation for a unified England.

**King Charles I:** This book looks at the reign of Charles I leading up to and during the English Civil War. It focuses on the religious and political conflicts between Charles I and Parliament, caused largely by

Charles' belief in divine right of kings and many unpopular, authoritarian policies. Abbott also examines Charles' refusal to compromise, leading to the war against Parliament's New Model Army and his eventual execution for treason in 1649 under Oliver Cromwell.

**King Charles II:** This biography deals with the restoration of the English monarchy under Charles II after the death of Oliver Cromwell. It follows Charles II's return from exile and re-establishment of royal power. However, Abbott also notes Charles' own conflicts with Parliament and religious controversies during his reign. The book discusses Charles' hedonistic lifestyle and many mistresses, but also his support for science, exploration and trade that helped expand the British Empire.

**Cleopatra:** This book examines Cleopatra VII's life and rule over ancient Egypt. Abbott chronicles Cleopatra's relationships and political alliances with Julius Caesar and Mark Antony, as she sought to maintain Egypt's independence from Rome. The biography highlights Cleopatra's intelligence, education and strategic skills in dealing with Rome. But it ultimately focuses on Cleopatra's downfall and suicide after Mark Antony's defeat by Octavian, leading to Egypt becoming a Roman province.

**Cyrus the Great:** This biography covers Cyrus II of Persia, founder of the Achaemenid Empire. Abbott traces Cyrus's rise from Persian prince, to revolt against the Medes, to conqueror of the Lydian and Babylonian empires. The book also examines Cyrus's leadership qualities and tolerant policies toward conquered peoples. It portrays Cyrus as a wise, inspirational leader who created the model of a centralized Persian state.

**Darius:** This book looks at the reign of Darius I, examining his consolidation of the Persian Empire through administrative reforms, development of infrastructure, and expansion of territory. Abbott discusses

Darius's división of the empire into provinces and implementation of a uniform tax system and coinage. The biography also covers his invasion of Greece which was thwarted at the famous Battle of Marathon. Overall, it presents Darius as an capable, pragmatic ruler under whom the Persian Empire reached its zenith.

**Queen Elizabeth:** This biography celebrates the long and prosperous reign of Queen Elizabeth I of England. Abbott focuses on Elizabeth's shrewd leadership, religious compromise, and patronage of the arts and literature that fostered English Renaissance culture. The book also highlights Elizabeth's naval defeat of the Spanish Armada which secured England's independence from Europe. Overall, Abbott portrays Elizabeth as a commanding, canny and popular female ruler who strengthened England as a major world power.

**Genghis Khan:** This book looks at the incredible rise of Temüjin, better known as Genghis Khan. It follows his hardships as an outcast youth to becoming the fearsome founder of the Mongol Empire. Abbott chronicles Genghis Khan's brilliant military tactics and utterly ruthless conquests that allowed the Mongols to dominate much of Asia and Eastern Europe. Overall it paints him as a complex figure--strategic genius but also brutal tyrant.

**Hannibal:** This biography focuses on the great Carthaginian general Hannibal Barca. It recounts his famous crossing of the Alps with war elephants and invasion of Italy during the Second Punic War against Rome. Abbott details Hannibal's victories in major battles like Cannae but also his eventual defeat by Scipio and exile. The book celebrates Hannibal's daring military prowess but also concession late in life that Rome could not be conquered.

**Josephine:** This book examines the life of Josephine Bonaparte from her aristocratic upbringing in Martinique to her marriage to Napoleon Bonaparte. It focuses on Josephine's time as Empress consort of France

| 163 |

and her support for arts and education. But it also discusses Napoleon's eventual divorce from her due to dynastic pressures. Overall the book presents Josephine as an intelligent, compassionate woman who tempered some of Napoleon's ambition.

**Julius Caesar:** This traces Caesar's life from early military campaigns to dictator and eventual assassination. Abbott covers Caesar's conquest of Gaul, rivalry with Pompey, famously crossing the Rubicon and crowning as dictator. The biography also examines the conspiracy led by Brutus and Cassius to assassinate Caesar in order to save the Roman Republic. In all, the book presents Caesar as an unmatched military mind who irrevocably changed the Roman Empire.

**Margaret of Anjou:** This biography looks at Margaret of Anjou who became queen consort to England's King Henry VI. It focuses on the political intrigue and machinations Margaret became involved in to support her husband's reign during the War of the Roses. Abbott portrays Margaret as a fiercely devoted, cunning woman who backed the Lancastrians against factions like the Yorkists led by Richard Neville. Though she lost power, the book frames her as a dominant figure during the conflict.

**Mary, Queen of Scots:** This book examines the life of Mary Stuart who became Queen of Scotland as an infant. It follows her tumultuous reign marked by scandals and plots to overthrow her by Protestants. Her Catholicism also put her at odds with England's Elizabeth I. Abbott recounts Mary's forced abdication, escape to England, and eventual execution ordered by Elizabeth for plotting against her. Overall it presents a tragic figure whose life was marked by political and religious turmoil.

**Nero:** This biography looks at the notorious Roman emperor Nero. It explores his self-indulgent lifestyle and tyrannical rule marked by possible matricide and the brutal execution of Christians. Abbott also examines legends around Nero like his fiddling during the Great Fire of Rome. The book presents a despotic, unstable man who drastically weakened the Roman Empire.

**Peter the Great:** This book covers the reforms and policies of Peter the Great that rapidly westernized Russia. Abbott discusses Peter's extensive European travels as a youth and later programs to remake Russia's army, expand its naval fleet, and build a new capital in St. Petersburg. The biography also examines Peter's harsh, authoritarian approach to governing that consolidated his power. Overall it presents him as a pivotal, transformative tsar.

**Pyrrhus:** This examines the life and military exploits of Pyrrhus, king of Epirus. It focuses on his campaigns against Rome where he won major battles but suffered heavy losses, giving rise to the term "Pyrrhic victory." Abbott recounts Pyrrhus's struggles to build a Greek empire and failed invasion of Sicily against Carthage. Though a skilled commander, Pyrrhus ultimately failed to achieve lasting gains.

**Richard I:** This biography looks at the reign of Richard I, known as Lionheart. It focuses on Richard's leadership during the Third Crusade to recapture Jerusalem from Saladin. Abbott also details the legendary tales of Richard's bravery and valor in campaigns against France and during his imprisonment. Overall, the book presents Richard I as one of England's great warrior kings.

**Richard II:** This explores the reign and overthrow of King Richard II. Abbott covers Richard's despotic actions that led the nobles to revolt and install Henry IV, leading to Richard's imprisonment and likely murder. The biography presents a weak king whose tyranny and poor leadership during a peasant's revolt cost him power and his life.

**Richard III:** This delves into the controversial rule of Richard III. Abbott examines Richard's contested path to the throne and the disappearance of the Princes in the Tower which Richard likely ordered. It also portrays Richard's defeat at the hands of Henry Tudor at the Battle of Bosworth Field that ended the Wars of the Roses. Ultimately Abbott paints Richard III as willing to employ any means to gain and retain the English crown.

**Romulus:** This recounts the Roman legend of Romulus and Remus, twin brothers raised by a she-wolf who went on to found the city of Rome. Abbott covers the myths of the brothers' quarrel over leadership, with Romulus killing Remus and becoming Rome's first king and architect of its nascent political institutions. Though mythological, Romulus represents ancient Rome's founding origins and rise to power.

**William the Conqueror:** This biography follows William, Duke of Normandy's conquest of England in 1066 after victory at the Battle of Hastings. Abbott discusses William's reign as king where he consolidated control, introduced feudalism, and fused English and Norman culture. William is presented as a formidable, innovative Norman leader who irrevocably transformed Anglo-Saxon England.

**Xerxes:** This examines the reign of Xerxes I of Persia, known for his failed invasion of Greece. Abbott focuses on Xerxes's gathering of a massive army to crush Greek resistance, but defeat at Salamis ended his ambitions. The book covers later unrest and palace intrigue that clouded the end of Xerxes's reign. Overall he is portrayed as a rash ruler whose desire for conquest led to disaster for Persia.

www.ingramcontent.com/pod-product-compliance
Lightning Source LLC
Chambersburg PA
CBHW070101080526
**44586CB00013B/1149**